To Jim and S̶̶̶̶ ♡
with thoughts of the lovely time
we had this summer.
1978.

John, Al·Louise, Susan,
and Beth Ramp

W9-BFQ-152

THROUGH TIME AND THE VALLEY

THROUGH TIME AND THE VALLEY

by JOHN R. ERICKSON

PHOTOGRAPHS by BILL ELLZEY

JACKET by VIC BLACKBURN

SHOAL CREEK PUBLISHERS, INC.

P.O. BOX 9737   AUSTIN, TEXAS 78766

COPYRIGHT © 1978 BY JOHN R. ERICKSON

All rights in this book are reserved. No part of this book may be used or reproduced in any manner whatsoever without written permission from the publisher, except in the case of brief quotations embedded in a review.

First Edition

LITHOGRAPHED AND BOUND IN THE UNITED STATES OF AMERICA

Library of Congress Cataloging in Publication Data

Erickson, John R.   , 1943–
Through time and the valley

Bibliography: p.
Includes index.
1. Canadian Valley, N.M.-Okla.-History.
2. Canadian Valley, N.M.-Okla.-Description and travel.
3. Erickson, John R., 1943–   I. Title.
F392.C27E74   1978
976.4'81   78-5320
ISBN 0-88319-036-2

DEDICATION

On May 20, 1977, I received a letter from Shoal Creek Publishers indicating that they might be interested in publishing *Through Time and the Valley*. That same day my mother died suddenly at the age of sixty-five. I deeply regret that, after reading to me when I was a child, teaching me the love of language, and telling me the tales of Martha Sherman and Grampy Buck and Uncles Roy and Bert and Tom Ross the outlaw, she did not live to see my first book.

I dedicate this book to her with fond memories and deepest appreciation. May my life and my writing always bring honor to her name.

AUTHOR'S NOTE

Through Time and the Valley deals with the segment of the Canadian River that passes through the ranch country in Hutchinson, Roberts, and Hemphill Counties of the Texas Panhandle. I am aware that another book, perhaps even two or three books, could be written about this same stretch of country. I could name a dozen ranchers whose names do not appear in the text and whose stories I never heard. I regret these omissions and can only say I wish I had had the time and the pages to record them all.

CONTENTS

ILLUSTRATIONS

ACKNOWLEDGMENTS

I must begin by acknowledging my debt to those Texas writers who blazed the trail and who have left young writers like me with a strong and viable literary tradition. The writings of J. Frank Dobie, J. Evetts Haley, John Graves, Al Dewlin, and Larry McMurtry have sustained and inspired me, given shape to my writing, and provided me with an example of high craftsmanship. Had they not pointed the way, it might never have occurred to me that Texas, and especially the Panhandle, could be a subject worthy of a young man's attention.

I am also indebted to the good and openhearted people of the Canadian River country who made this work possible:

The ranchers and landowners along the river who gave Bill Ellzey and me permission to cross their country—J. A. Whittenburg III, Bud Brainard, George Arrington, Leroy McGarraugh, Albert McGarraugh, Scott McGarraugh, Cliff McGarraugh, Walter Killebrew, Jim Streeter, Frank McMordie, Hugh Parsell, Ben Hill, Tom Conatser, W. A. McQuiddy, and John Isaacs;

The families who took us into their homes during our ride down the river—Mr. and Mrs. Ed Brainard,

Mr. and Mrs. Ben McIntyre, Mr. and Mrs. Leroy McGarraugh, Jim Streeter, Mr. and Mrs. David Trimble, Ben and Arnold Hill, Tom Conatser, Mr. and Mrs. Hunky Green, Mr. and Mrs. John Isaacs, and Mr. and Mrs. Ben Ezzell;

And the storytellers and yarn-spinners who shared their tales with me, and whose names appear at the back of the book.

I also wish to express my thanks to the following people who contributed to the making of this book:

Ed Atkinson of Perryton who aided me in legal research;

The Ellzey family of Wolf Creek, especially Lawrence, whose list of favors and services would run to several pages;

Bill Herndon, also of Wolf Creek, who loaned us Dobbin Mule for the river trip;

Paul F. Boller, Jr., of Fort Worth who, in 1963, began telling me, "You learn to write by writing," and has given me encouragement ever since;

Bill Ellzey, my partner in this adventure; as the old-timers used to say, "He'll do to ride the river with";

Judy Timberg, my kind and patient editor at Shoal Creek Publishers;

Joe and Anna Beth Erickson, my parents;

And my wife, Kris Erickson, who has sustained me through ten long years of rejection slips, and given me life.

A couple of old-timers in the Canadian River valley. Windmills brought water to the West and made large-scale ranching possible. Cottonwood trees have been native to the valley for centuries. The old cottonwood shown here was blown down two weeks after this photo was taken.

I

The Canadian River of Texas
June, 1972

"You can comprehend a piece of a river.
A whole river that is really a river is
much to comprehend."
                    —John Graves, *Goodbye to A River*

It was summer. It was June. It was the morning of the day
we began our journey through time and the valley.

Bill Ellzey and I watched as the pickup and stock trailer
climbed the last fifty yards of caliche road and disappeared over
the rim of the caprock, leaving behind a haze of white dust and
a silence that spread from horizon to horizon. We were alone
now, just the two of us, with two horses and a mule and enough
dried food to keep us alive for fifteen days.

We had come to the old ghost town of Plemons to begin a
fifteen-day horseback trip down the river, which would take
us to the Oklahoma border and then back to the town of
Canadian. It was not going to be a casual ride or just a camping
expedition. Bill and I had been preparing for it for almost a
year. It was our intention to experience "a piece of a river," as
John Graves put it, and to record the characters and stories,
the beauty and flavor of an isolated region in the northeastern

1

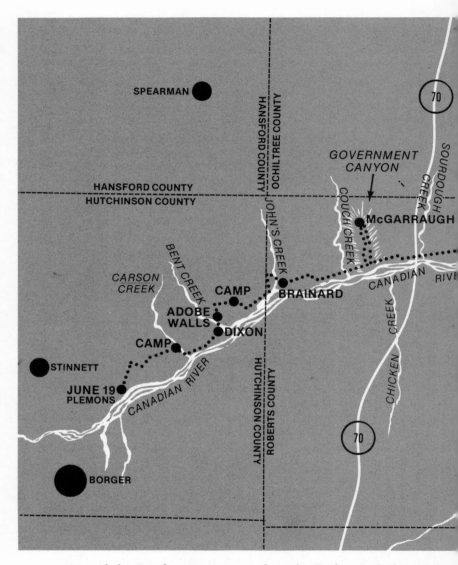

Map of the Canadian River trip. Author John Erickson and photographer Bill Ellzey traveled east across the Texas Panhandle for fifteen days. They rode 140 miles on horseback through Hutchinson, Roberts, and Hemphill

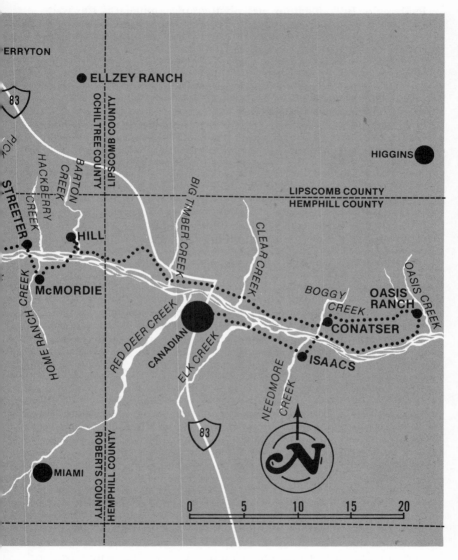

Counties. The places they camped and the people they stayed with are noted in large type.

Panhandle. Bill's medium was photography, mine was the written word, and this book is the fruit of our labors.

My material was not gathered entirely on the trip. By the time I climbed on my horse that morning in Plemons, I had spent many hours in libraries, newspaper files, and courthouses all over the Panhandle, trying to bring together everything that had been written about the Canadian River between Borger and the Oklahoma line. That in itself would have made a slim volume, however, because from a strictly historical point of view, not much has happened here in the last three hundred years. Nor did I want to write a book that was strictly historical. I wanted to get the facts, but I also wanted to get out of the library, see the country from horseback, and meet the people as I found them. For that reason, I conducted about a hundred interviews in the field between August of 1971 and July of 1972.

What I gathered in these interviews was something less than scholastic history and something more than common gossip. Perhaps "yarns" would be the best word for it. I would not care to blur the distinction between history and yarn, because there is a place for both—and I have used both in this book. I suppose we could say that history is that body of knowledge which can be verified by written records and tangible artifacts, while a yarn carries only the authority of the storyteller. If his memory is good, then the yarn may be historically correct; if his memory is poor, or if his imagination is active, the yarn may prove entertaining though not necessarily accurate. I have tried to follow history as far as it would go, and have provided chapter notes at the back to document these labors. But where history has stopped, I have not hesitated to use yarns, and to me the yarns are just as important as the history. While facts and dates capture an event and hold it in a particular time and place, yarns are timeless. They add flavor and spice to what might otherwise be a tiresome recital of data, and provide us with living flesh to cover the bones of fact.

If yarns are not history, neither are they a poor substitute for history. They have their own function and integrity. If it is the function of history to inform, then it is the function of yarns to entertain. We should not expect history to entertain in all instances or yarns to give us scientific data. Once we understand the value and limits of each, then we can employ both to describe a people and a place, and our final impression will be more complete than if we had relied on just one or the other.

One final word on the yarns in this book. I grew up in Perryton, thirty miles north of the river, and yet in my youth I never heard any of the stories I relate here. Though I suspected that a rich folklore had grown up amid the magnificent isolation of the Canadian, I did not know just how rich it was until I devoted a year of my life to seeking it out. I suspect that very few, and perhaps none of the yarns I collected have ever been heard by people who have not lived along the river. It was my privilege to hear them, and it is my privilege now to give them to other generations and to readers who may never have seen the Canadian River. I can take credit only for writing them down, and for being in a position to hear them from the old-timers before death stole them away.

So there we were in Plemons, Bill Ellzey and I, with a hundred and forty miles of horseback riding before us. Bill's horse was a gray gelding named Suds, a tall handsome quarter horse that had come out of the mare band on the LZ Ranch in Ochiltree County. Bill worked on the LZ Ranch, which belonged to his uncle Lawrence Ellzey, and had bought Suds and broke him to ride. At three, Suds had a nice disposition and promised to make a fine saddlehorse, but he was still young and excitable, and Bill felt that the long trip down the river would do him a lot of good.

I was riding a bay gelding named Dollarbill. Lawrence Ellzey had bought him for me at a livestock sale in Oklahoma. Dollarbill was about twelve years old when I purchased him, and he was what you would call a nice $150 horse—which is to say that he had his flaws. He was short-coupled, a painfully slow walker, and rather mule-faced; he had a few stubborn habits and was slothful until spurred. But he was gentle and not given to much mischief, and I was not so much a horseman then that I overlooked those good qualities. He was good enough for whom he was carrying.

Bill and I had come prepared to camp out for fifteen nights, and had brought the least amount of equipment necessary for survival and small comfort. We carried our bedrolls, wrapped in rain slickers, behind our saddles, and the rest was packed in duffle bags which we heaped upon a mule named Dobbin. Included in our equipment were: a pup tent, a lantern, canteens, waterbags, cooking utensils, an ax, a canvas tarp, and food. Ours was strictly a survival ration, composed primarily of rice, jerked beef, dried fruit, slab bacon, and flour.

The big canyon country of the Canadian River valley. Author Erickson calls these the most spectacular escarpments of the northeastern Panhandle. This photo, taken between Perryton and Pampa, shows Battleship Rock rising in the background.

Dobbin the mule was one of the imponderables of the trip. Bill Herndon, a rancher on Wolf Creek south of Perryton, had graciously offered us the use of Dobbin, and though we had worked with him to some extent before the trip began, we had an uncomfortable feeling about him. Neither Bill Ellzey nor I had had any previous experience with mules, and we didn't know exactly what to expect. Our feeling was that, while horses are fairly predictable, mules are fairly unpredictable. We had practiced loading our gear on Dobbin and had led him behind a horse. He had performed without protest, but with an air of silent rebellion. What he would do out in the middle of the big ranch country, we did not know.

There, in the old ghost town of Plemons, with the silence of the Canadian River valley all around us, we were alone with our thoughts and the piece of river we had set out to meet. There is a certain irony involved in any romance with the Canadian River, because one must first decide exactly what it is. On the map, it is a ribbon of blue that begins near Costilla Peak in the Sangre de Cristo range of northern New Mexico. It enters Texas in Oldham County, snakes across the Panhandle into Oklahoma, and there joins the Arkansas on its journey to the Gulf of Mexico. But beyond that, what is it? Does a river begin up on the flats where the plains break into gentle hills and water-carrying draws? Or at the caprock where the prairie suddenly drops two hundred feet to the canyon bottoms below? Or is it the wide valley from caprock to caprock? Or maybe the creeks and feeder streams that cross the valley from north and south? Or is a river simply the water that flows from cutbank to cutbank?

To someone from Missouri or Ohio, this line of questioning might seem trivial, for in those parts a river is what a bridge goes across, which inevitably is *water*. But if a river implies water, then the Canadian River does not exist at certain times of the year; or, even more perverse, it may exist for a mile, then cease to exist, then re-exist five miles below. Depending on the weather upstream, the Canadian may be a boiling cataract, a timid little creek that you can jump across, or nothing more than a wide bed of sand.

So what is the Canadian River? That is what Bill and I had set out to discover. From Plemons we would follow her for a hundred and forty miles, from the river bottom to the canyon country, from the lush meadows of the Turkey Track Ranch to the redland prairies of the Oasis Ranch, from the ghost town of Plemons to the little cowtown of Canadian.

This is the story of our trip. But more importantly, it is the story of the people who have lived and died there and left behind some yarns to pass on to the next generation. And in the end, that's all a river is: not water, but people and stories.

Author Erickson, mounted on Dollarbill, "the best $150 horse in the Panhandle," leads Dobbin the pack mule down the Canadian River valley.

II

Shine Popejoy

The Texas Panhandle is a very young country, and like most young countries it has spawned an inordinately large number of ghost towns: Old Ochiltree, Old Hansford, Sweetwater, Taz, Zulu, Timm's City, Hogtown, Parnell, Tascosa, Oil City, GeWhitt, and Plemons, to name but a few.

Around 1895, Plemons appeared in a lovely little valley on the north bank of the Canadian River, about a mile south of the caprock. In 1901 an election was held, Plemons won the county seat of Hutchinson County, and a courthouse was erected on Main Street. Later came a post office, boardinghouses, two general stores, and a doctor. By 1920 Plemons had taken a good strong grip on the prairie, and its future as a town seemed secure.

Then in 1926, the Dixon Creek Oil Company discovered oil on the Smith Ranch near the river. Drilling crews filled the boardinghouses at Plemons and it appeared that the boom would make a city. But promoters had come to the country and were driving stakes and pushing the new towns of Borger and Stinnett, and that is where the boom went. When the Rock Island passed up Plemons and built a line into Stinnett, Plemons's doom had been sealed. Another election was called and the county seat went to Stinnett, and when the residents of Plemons threatened a court suit, the newly elected county commissioners held a midnight meeting, backed a truck up to the courthouse in Plemons, and drove off to Stinnett with all the county records.

9

Plemons, once the county seat of Hutchinson County, died when the oil boom of the Twenties and Thirties went to the town of Borger across the river. Today, the old Plemons cemetery lies all but forgotten on a private ranch in the Canadian River valley.

Bill Ellzey and I spent an hour poking around what is left of Plemons, which now lies abandoned on a private ranch north of Borger. The courthouse and most of the homes had been moved elsewhere, and those that remained were slowly rotting into the ground.

The discovery of oil radically changed the complexion of Hutchinson County. Towns with names like Signal Hill, Electric City, Oil City, and GeWhitt bloomed and withered like prairie flowers after a spring rain. Wooden derricks, pump jacks, and tank batteries sprang up on the mesquite hills along the Canadian River, and streams of black crude oil oozed down the sandy draws. In six months, Borger swelled into a tent and sheet iron city of fifty thousand. (It has been estimated that 3,500 of the citizens were prostitutes and dance hall girls.) Drillers, salesmen, speculators, and promoters poured in from the boom towns of Oklahoma and East Texas, and right behind them came some of the toughest hoodlums in the Southwest: Yellow Young, Ray Terrill, Spider Gibson, Wireline Yerkey, and Shine Popejoy. A good deal has been written about the promoters and speculators who made their fortunes in the oil fields of Texas, so let us turn our attention to the second group and spin a few yarns from the life of Shine Popejoy.

Johnny Waltine Popejoy was born in Huntsville, Arkansas, in 1885 and came to manhood in Henryetta, Oklahoma, a part of the world which had already spawned more than its share of outlaws. In 1905 he married Rosie Bruner, a full-blooded Choctaw Indian, and when she died at the birth of their second child, Shine placed the children with relatives and began to roam. Since he had never cared much for sweat-of-the-brow forms of work, he turned to gambling, robbing, bootlegging, and moonshining. It was from this last category that he acquired the name Shine.

Mozell Eslin, Shine's only daughter, first learned of her father's activities when she was very young. One day while playing in the front yard, she looked up and saw a cloud of dust coming up the road. A moment later Shine's steaming automobile slid to a stop in front of the house. Leaping out of the car, he pointed to a pile of canvas bags in the back seat and shouted, "Grab the sacks, daughter, they're after me!" He had just held up the Henryetta post office.

Mrs. Eslin recalled another story about her notorious father. It seems Shine had hired a tight-lipped old man to operate one

11

of his stills around Henryetta. This faithful old man served his boss well until he came down with a hacking cough and grew so weak he could hardly get around. When a doctor diagnosed the malady as consumption, the old fellow went to Shine and told him about it.

"What are you going to do?" Shine asked.

The old man shook his head. "I just want to die, that's all. I'm no good to you or anybody else anymore." He looked his boss straight in the eye. "Shine, I'd like for you to put me out of my misery. I've thought it over and that's what I want. Will you do it?"

Shine stood there for a moment, studying the old man's face. Then he shrugged. "All right, if that's what you want. Where do you want to be put?" Since he had no family and no money for a cemetery plot, he said that Shine's back yard would be fine. When he had dug his own grave, Shine gave him enough money to buy a casket, and when all the arrangements had been made, Shine shot him and buried him in the back yard.

In relating this story, Mrs. Eslin explained that the incident never bothered her father in later years. "He was cold-blooded. He could have shot one of his own children and not felt bad about it."

In 1926 Shine heard about the oil boom in the Texas Panhandle. Since federal Prohibition had dried up the supply of legal whiskey, he figured fifty thousand thirsty roughnecks in Hutchinson County would provide a lucrative market for his moonshine. From the Blue Moon, a bootleg joint he opened in Stinnett on the north side of the river, he operated his business empire, which by this time had grown to include prostitution. Here, wearing a white Stetson hat, a diamond stick pin, and a pair of pearl-handled .45 pistols, flashing his four gold teeth and searching the crowd with a pair of pale blue eyes, he reigned like a king in his castle.

Shine established himself quickly in this new setting. He wasted no time getting on the good side of the law officers, and he went to great lengths to cultivate them. Exactly how far he went is not clear. Perhaps he got into their good graces through friendship alone, but in light of the corruption of local officials that was exposed in 1929 (which we shall examine in greater detail later on), it would not be too farfetched to suppose that he was paying them off on the side.

Shine also developed quite a following among the citizens of Stinnett, Signal Hill, and the other little towns north of the river, many of whom regarded him as a modern version of Robin Hood. It was said that no friend of Shine Popejoy ever went hungry. A man down on his luck could go to Shine at any hour of the day or night and get a loan, with no questions asked and no papers signed.

This is not to say, however, that he never had trouble with people. Occasionally at the Blue Moon a fellow would drink too much and get out of hand, in which case Shine administered his own brand of justice. The offender was taken to a little sheet iron building behind the Blue Moon, clapped into neck irons attached to a railroad tie, and left until he sobered up.

Shine also made some bitter enemies, and after spending one peaceful and prosperous year in Stinnett, he encountered trouble from two sources: a man named Bill Parks, and the Texas Rangers.

Parks worked for Popejoy as a bootlegger. Early in 1927 Shine discovered that his man was stealing whiskey and selling it out of his own little joint in Electric City. On March 10, while Shine was hauling a load of whiskey to Borger, Parks, Bob Hannah, and two other men ran his truck off the road, robbed him, and shot him in the head. The bullet struck him in the middle of the forehead, but instead of penetrating the skull, it traveled upward, leaving a bloody wound in its path and passing through the sweatband of his Stetson hat.

Shine crumpled to the floor and played dead, listening as Parks laid his plot for disposing of the body. The men decided to take him into one of the isolated canyons along the river, cover the body with gasoline, and set it on fire. Shine waited for his chance to escape. When the men stopped in GeWhitt to fill a five-gallon can with gas, he jumped out of the car and disappeared into the night.

On March 26 a new Buick coupe pulled up in front of the Stinnett post office. A neatly dressed man in a white hat reached behind the seat, pulled out a sawed-off shotgun, and walked into the post office. The man was Shine Popejoy, and he had come to make his final settlement with Bill Parks, who was buying stamps at the window. Shine raised the shotgun. "Bill, I've been looking for you. Turn around." When Parks turned, the first blast struck him full in the chest. Dazed and bleeding, he staggered to the door where Shine gave him the second

13

barrel and blew the top of his head out into the street. Shine stepped over the body, walked to his car, and drove away.

He was indicted for murder and the case came to trial on April 14. Because of the notoriety of the killing, the trial was moved to neighboring Roberts County on a change of venue. Arguing that Parks had deserved killing, the defense lawyers produced Shine's Stetson hat as evidence that Parks had tried to murder him. When the jury saw that the hole in the hat perfectly matched the scar on Shine's forehead, they returned a verdict of not guilty.[1]

But by this time Shine had other problems to worry about. On April 8, 1927, while he was under indictment for Parks's murder, a squad of Texas Rangers (including Frank Hamer, whose name will appear later in the story) raided a Popejoy still and charged him with violation of Prohibition laws. This still, located north of Stinnett, was built entirely underground and could be reached only by a narrow mule trail which led to a small cave-like opening. The operation was so well concealed that the Rangers only found it when an airborne spotter noticed a curl of smoke drifting up from the hills.

But in spite of his problems in 1927, Shine managed to stay out of jail. The Rangers moved on to other trouble spots in Texas, and business in Hutchinson County returned to its normal state. Fortunes in oil were pumped out of the ground, thousands of gallons of illegal whiskey bubbled away in the canyons along the river, and the corruption of public officials continued at a brisk pace. But by the year 1929, the winds of change were beginning to stir. A young and vigorous district attorney, John A. Holmes, began going after the moonshiners and left everyone with the impression that he intended to clean up Hutchinson County. In July Shine Popejoy suffered his first setback in two years when he was arrested for possessing and transporting intoxicating liquor. On September 15 John Holmes spent the day putting the finishing touches on fourteen liquor cases he intended to prosecute in federal district court. That evening he was murdered in his front yard by an assassin whose identity remains a mystery to this day.

The audacity of the killing sent a quiver through the entire state of Texas. Governor Dan Moody expressed outrage at the crime, and within three days he had dispatched a squad of Texas Rangers and special prosecutor Clem Calhoun to the troubled city of Borger. On September 22 Ranger Captain

14

Frank Hamer, the same officer who had led the raid on Shine Popejoy's still two years before, brought this report to the Governor: "Hutchinson County possesses the worst organized crime ring I have observed in my twenty-three years as a Texas Ranger. Many of the officers of the law are either ex-convicts or under indictment of criminal offenses at the present time."

Three days later, Governor Moody issued this statement: "There exists a conspiracy between officers and the criminal element, and there have been obtained affidavits of instances of money passing to peace officers for protection from enforcement of the law. The peace officers for some reason are failing to suppress crime and bring criminals to justice."

Those were harsh words, and the Governor backed them up with actions to match. On September 20 one hundred and fourteen men and officers of the Texas National Guard arrived in Borger on the morning train, and at 9 a.m. Borger and Hutchinson County were placed under martial law. Troops occupied all county and city offices, and under General Order Number 6 law violators were detained in jail without bond. Among the first to be detained were Clint Millhollon, Borger police officer, and Deputy Constable Sam Jones, the latter charged with accepting bribes. By the time martial law was lifted on October 30, the county had seen the resignation of every major official, including Sheriff Joe Ownbey, Mayor Pace of Borger, all the city commissioners, six police officers, and a state representative.[2]

We don't know to what extent the reforms affected Shine Popejoy, but court records indicate that for the next two years he lived in Obar, New Mexico, on two hundred acres of land. This would seem to suggest that the reform movement hit him hard, in fact probably closed down his Texas operations entirely. One detects a certain desperation in his actions on his return to Texas, as if, deprived of his "legitimate" business of moonshining, he has turned to more serious forms of crime.

On March 15, 1932, G. W. Newsome, president of the First State Bank of Stinnett, drove to Borger to pick up a shipment of money. On his return, he was stopped by Shine Popejoy, who poked a gun in his face and made off with $4,657 in cash. A month later Shine was charged with armed robbery. In the meantime, he was brought to trial on the 1929 charge of possessing and transporting liquor. The jury found him guilty and assessed punishment of two years in the state penitentiary. His lawyers first sought a new trial, then vowed to appeal the decision to a higher court.

The hand of the law was closing in on Shine, but he wasn't through yet. On November 15, while out on bail on the charge of armed robbery and awaiting the higher court's opinion on the liquor conviction, he robbed the Stinnett bank again, this time with the aid of Joe Wolfe, Jelly Stewart, and W. H. Burke. Less than a week later he was arrested in a private home in Oklahoma City. Officers found two pearl-handled .45 pistols in his lap and $216 in his pocket, which he claimed to have earned picking cotton near Carnegie, Oklahoma. So once again Shine saw the inside of the Hutchinson County jail, and this time it appeared he would be there for a long time.[3]

On January 15, 1933, jailer Dan Cambern and his son DeWitt were in the jail picking up dishes after the prisoners had eaten supper. Cambern told the *Borger Daily Herald*,

> DeWitt and I went in around 4:30. I opened the door and Henry Letterman, one of the prisoners, handed me an empty tray. I had given orders that the prisoners always were to stay out of the runway. I think Shine came out of the second cell. He came out like a flash and faced me and as he came around the door he shot me in the fleshy part of the left leg.
>
> DeWitt was directly behind me and when Popejoy fired DeWitt grabbed his right arm, caught him around the neck, and turned him around so that his side was toward me. DeWitt had no gun, and I was afraid the rest of the prisoners would come.
>
> While he was fighting DeWitt like a tiger, I fired the shots. He tried to turn his gun on DeWitt. They wrestled to the floor right in the doorway and I had to pick my time and place to shoot. At one time he had his gun nearly up to shoot DeWitt. Right before I fired the fifth shot he looked up at me and said, 'You —— ——!'

Shine Popejoy died that afternoon on the floor of the county jail. According to law officers, he had lowered a rope out the window and someone on the outside had tied a .32 Derringer, a .45 pistol, and four hacksaw blades to the end of it. Mrs. Lois Marsh of Pampa, Texas, Dan Cambern's daughter, told me that another prisoner was supposed to come out shooting with Popejoy, but that for some reason he did not.

16

Ironically, Shine and the bank he robbed twice died only two days apart. On January 13 the beleaguered G. W. Newsome locked the door of the First State Bank of Stinnett and moved to another town.

❉ ❉ ❉

From Plemons, Bill Ellzey and I rode north, past the old cemetery which occupies a lonely spot on a hill overlooking the valley. We stopped for a few minutes and walked among the graves, some of which had been tended recently enough to be adorned with plastic flowers, others long since reclaimed by native grass and weeds. I had hoped to find an inscription that might reveal a story about the wild days when Shine Popejoy was making whiskey in this valley, but the epitaphs proved as stark as the setting.[4]

Erickson cooks dinner at the first night's camp on Carson Creek. The creek was named after Kit Carson, who in 1864 led a force of soldiers down the Canadian River Valley and was surprised by one of the largest armies of Plains Indians ever assembled.

III

Carson Creek

About six hours later we came to a spring of live water, a welcome sight after a long afternoon in the saddle. The air had been still and steamy along our course, and we had been pursued every step of the way by hordes of deer flies, a grayish insect about three times the size of a house fly. These loathsome creatures had the bite of an ice pick and drove our horses to distraction. Bill and I spent most of the day slapping flies on the necks of Suds and Dollarbill, and when we arrived at the spring on Carson Creek, our hands were covered with blood.

We left the horses hobbled in a lush green meadow and made our camp in a hackberry grove beside the creek. While Bill went back to the meadow to doctor a gall on the mule, I kindled a fire and put the evening meal on to cook: rice and jerked beef simmered in bouillon broth, fried bacon, raisins, and sassafras tea. Jerked beef, once a staple in the diet of pioneers, can now be purchased in almost any quick-stop grocery store. I made our jerky from a recipe given to me by my grandmother, the late Mrs. B. B. Curry of Seminole, Texas. One summer evening, as we were sitting on her front porch, she told me about her childhood in the old Quaker community of Estacado in Crosby County, where she often saw strips of beef hanging on lines to dry in the sun.

When Bill returned from the meadow, we spread a slicker on the ground beside the fire and sat down to a good hot meal.

19

The jerky lacked the taste and flavor of the roast from which it had come, but we found it filling and satisfying. After supper, we nursed cups of hot sassafras tea and watched the sun slide behind a hill, until our growing shadows reminded us that we had chores to do before dark. Ordinarily, we would have pitched the tent, dug a trench around it, and covered our saddles with the tarp—normal precautions against rain. But it was a beautiful evening, without a cloud in the sky, and we decided that it could not possibly rain in the night. As a hedge against this prediction, we pitched the tent, though we did not bother to trench around it or roll out our bedding inside. We would sleep under the stars. As the cloak of night wrapped itself around the land, we crawled into our blankets on the banks of Carson Creek.

✿ ✿ ✿

It was in the winter of 1864 that Colonel Christopher (Kit) Carson marched his men from Cimarron, New Mexico, to the creek in the Texas Panhandle which now bears his name.

During the Civil War, the government in Washington had been forced to withdraw most of its troops from the frontier garrisons on the Southern Plains and to throw them into the war against the Confederacy. The Kiowas, Comanches, Southern Cheyennes, and Arapahoes, by this time allied against the expansion of white civilization, took full advantage of the withdrawal. They attacked military posts and wagon trains in Kansas, pillaged the settlements below the Red River in Texas, and left the whole country in a state of panic. By the middle of 1864, Washington was flooded with reports of shocking depredations, and the decision was made to punish the Indians.

Kit Carson, who had already distinguished himself as a scout under John Charles Frémont and as commander of the summer campaign against the Navahos, received his orders in October to march to the Canadian River to punish hostile Kiowas and Comanches, reported to be in their winter camps along the river valley. On November 6, Carson left Cimarron with 350 mounted men, 70 Ute and Apache scouts (some with wives), 27 wagons, and 2 mountain howitzers.

On November 24, Carson's Indian scouts, enveloped in buffalo robes to protect themselves against the bitter cold, reported finding an encampment of one hundred and seventy-six teepees down the river. Carson ordered a night march to get his force within striking distance of the village, and early the next morning they attacked. In the first wave were the Utes and Apaches, wearing only their paint and feathers in the extreme cold. As Carson's army advanced toward the village, the Kiowas fled in the opposite direction, the women and children to the hills, and the warriors downstream toward a large Comanche village four miles to the east. The soldiers entered the camp and began mopping up. The Indians who had not escaped—the old and sick—were executed by the Utes and Apaches. Then the Ute and Apache women fell to the grisly task of mutilating the bodies.

It appeared that Carson had scored a decisive victory, and he issued the command to burn the village.

But there were several factors he had not counted on. The first was the huge Comanche camp downriver. The second involved a Kiowa chief named Dohasan. It was Dohasan's village that the soldiers were intent on destroying.

After covering the retreat of the women and children, Dohasan and his men whipped their horses down the wide Canadian valley toward the Comanche camp. He must have felt the sting of humiliation as he galloped away, for he had not established himself as head chief of the Kiowas on his ability to run away from a fight. Stealing quick glances at the faces of his men, his mind drifted back to the year 1833.

The Kiowa calendar identified 1833 as "The Year They Cut Off Our Heads," and if you were a Kiowa you couldn't speak of that year without feeling sick at heart. It was in the summer. Adate, the head chief at the time, had taken all the warriors out on a hunting expedition, leaving the women, children, and old people unguarded in camp. While the men were away, a party of Osages, blood enemies of the Kiowa tribe, fell upon the camp and massacred all the women who weren't able to escape. When the Kiowa warriors returned home, they found their camp in ruins and the heads of their wives stuffed into cooking pots. Adate was stripped of his rank on the spot, and Dohasan, a young and brave warrior, was elevated to head chief.

Dohasan remembered the ceremony. He had been tall and erect then, his fine head framed by long braids ornamented with silver brooches that reached to his knees. He had come to the ceremony dressed in his finest: a boar's tusk and an eagle bone whistle around his neck, a mantle of red Spanish cloth, fringed leggings, and wide copper bands on his arms.

21

In the years since, he had tried to be a good chief. He had represented his people at the peace table with the white soldiers in 1837. Then in 1840, when war became inevitable, he had formed an alliance with the five major tribes of Indians on the plains, a peace that had not been broken in twenty-four years. On long winter evenings, he had often looked back on his accomplishments with pride, but now he felt only the crushing weight of responsibility that went with his position. In the distance he heard the crack of a rifle, and then another, as more of his people died in the village, and the memory of the Osage Massacre and the disgrace of Adate swept through his mind.

"*Hood-le-ty!*" he cried to his men. "Hurry! Hurry!"

At the Comanche camp they sounded the alarm. While Dohasan and Stumbling Bear rode down the line shouting encouragement to the Kiowas, One-Eyed Bear rallied his Comanche warriors. In less than an hour, Dohasan looked out on what seemed an ocean of warriors, estimated by historians to have been between a thousand and five thousand well armed men. Their bows were strung, their rifles cocked, and their horses were snorting steam in the chilly air. It was the largest gathering of warriors he had ever seen.

Dohasan gave the sign, and suddenly they were flying across the prairie. He felt the big gray stud beneath him getting low to the ground and reaching out with his powerful legs. The wind stung his cheeks and the sound of the warriors filled his ears. He felt good. The aches in his joints disappeared. The old wounds that plagued him every winter suddenly healed. It was for this lightning charge across the prairie that Dohasan had been born. That's all a Kiowa could ask of life: a fleet horse, a good rifle, and an enemy to kill.

Dohasan and his men fought bravely that day. The battle raged through the morning and into the afternoon. Though neither side suffered heavy casualties, by three in the afternoon Kit Carson realized that his position was deteriorating by the minute. Twelve years later, George Armstrong Custer faced similar odds at the Little Big Horn. He elected to stay and fight. Carson took one look at the superior force of Indians and gave the order to retreat. Later, Carson wrote that he had never seen a more impressive display of daring and bravery than that of Dohasan's warriors. Historians have taken the compliment one step further by pointing out that had the retreat not been covered by cannon fire, Carson's force would very likely have been cut to pieces.[1]

❖ ❖ ❖

In our bedrolls on Carson Creek one hundred and eight years later, Bill Ellzey and I faced an attack of another sort. At dusk, the still steamy bottom along the creek came alive with clouds of hungry mosquitoes. The insect dope we had applied to our arms, necks, and faces kept the tormentors from biting, but not from hovering and buzzing in our ears. Just as I dropped off to sleep, I awakened to the sound of a P-38 flying through my ear canal. Cursing, I sat up.

"Bill," I said, intending to ask where he had put the mosquito dope. But before I could utter another word, I sucked one of the buzzing devils down my windpipe.

"Huh?" came my partner's groggy reply.

"Forget it," I choked, and went back to bed.

After hours of this torture, nature granted us sleep. By absorbing the mosquitoes into our dreams and converting them into airplanes and buzz saws, we managed to ignore them. We had been asleep for thirty minutes when the first raindrop exploded on the end of my nose. I sat straight up and heard the slap-slap of rain in the hackberry tree above us. By this time Bill had joined me. There wasn't much we could say. We had dared predict the weather in the Panhandle, and as is usually the case, we had guessed wrong.

We sprang into action—if that's what you call running into each other, kicking at blankets that have suddenly become pythons around your legs, stumbling over tent ropes, and walking your face into tree limbs. By the light of two fireflies down by the creek, we prepared our camp for the storm. While Bill tarped the saddles and gear, I started trenching around the tent, which I was not able to see in the darkness.

Finally, we dived into the tent and settled back into our beds, ready to be lulled to sleep by the patter of raindrops. We both agreed that, although a rain storm was something of an inconvenience, it would at least keep the mosquitoes at bay. The rain continued for a good five minutes. Then it stopped dead. In the silence, we heard squadrons of mosquitoes taking off from bases in the swamp grass along the creek, their radars blipping in our direction.

Billy Dixon, one of the pioneers in the Texas Panhandle, lived for twenty years on his ranch in Hutchinson County, until his losses in the cattle business forced him to sell the ranch and move to Plemons. In 1883 he planted one of the first orchards in the northern Panhandle, and when Erickson and Ellzey stopped at the old Dixon place in 1972, they found these four gnarled pear trees.

IV

Billy Dixon

The next day we rose at the crack of mid-morning, broke camp, and with our heads still fuzzed with all the sleep we didn't get, we made our way to the Billy Dixon place, three or four miles east.

In 1883 Billy Dixon resigned his position as scout at Ft. Elliott, Texas, and retired to a quieter life. Only thirty-three, he had seen more excitement than most men could have managed in a hundred years. He had whacked bull teams in Kansas, sat in on the Medicine Lodge Treaty of 1867, hunted buffalo from the Republican to the Canadian Rivers, fought in the Battle of Adobe Walls, and received the Congressional Medal of Honor for his part in the Battle of Buffalo Wallow. Now what he wanted most was to acquire some land and settle down to a quiet life in a good country.

Dixon had hunted and scouted over an enormous area in his lifetime, from northern Kansas to the Palo Duro Canyon in Texas, from the New Mexico line to Indian Territory. He knew every creek and spring, and could discourse on the taste of the water, the quality of the grass, and the amount of timber on each. Out of all this country he chose to settle on Bent's Creek in Hutchinson County, Texas, not only because it was a lovely spot, but also because from Bent's Creek he could look a mile and a half to the north and see the ruins of Adobe Walls. Adobe Walls had a special significance for Dixon, for it was there that he had first proved himself a man of uncommon ability and courage. Bat Masterson, who had fought with him at the Walls, had gone East to work for a New York newspaper after the battle and had written of Dixon's amazing shot, when he had knocked an Indian off his horse at a distance of seven-eighths of a mile. Now people all over the country knew the name Billy Dixon, and they associated it with Adobe Walls.

So in 1883 he returned to his heart's country, filed on three sections of land, and set to work improving his holdings. He built a small cabin, diverted the waters of Bent's Creek for irrigation, and planted an orchard of two hundred trees, probably the first ever to appear on the plains of the northern Panhandle. "Mine was a happy life in my cabin at Adobe Walls," he wrote years later, "without fret or worry, and with abundance of everything for my simple needs."[1] One gets the impression he would have been quite content to grow old there, tending his orchard, living on what he could hunt and raise, and taking his place among the heroes of the Panhandle.

But if man had been created with nothing but "simple needs," Father Adam would still be occupying the Garden of Eden, and the rest of us would never have been born. Dixon lived for nine years in his Eden, and then one morning he awoke with a strange feeling: it occurred to him for the first time that Billy Dixon, buffalo hunter, Indian fighter, and Joshua of the Texas Panhandle, was lonely.

Shortly thereafter, he met a pretty young school teacher named Olive King. One evening Billy tried to explain to Dutch and Fly, his faithful dogs, the strange feeling that crept into his breast every time he saw Miss Olive.

"Dutch, when the Indians had us surrounded at Buffalo Wallow, I looked eternity straight in the eyes and didn't even flinch, but when I do the same to Miss Olive . . . boys, I flinch and I quiver and get to feeling kind of faint. Now, there's something wrong when a man forty-three years old can't look at a young lady without falling to pieces. It ain't natural. But what do you do about it, Fly? I mean, you can't shoot her, and you can't ride her, and you can't give her a lickin'. Beats me."

With the dogs snoring contentedly at his feet, Billy stared into the fire for over an hour. Then he sighed and nodded his head.

"Dutch, I . . ." Lost in sleep, Dutch quivered and wheezed and rolled his eyeballs. Billy frowned and gave the dog a kick.

"Wake up, damn you, I've got something to say." Dutch roused himself from his dreams, then Fly sat up too. Billy waited until he was sure they were both wide awake. Then he announced with great dignity, "Boys, I guess I'll ask Miss Olive to marry me." The dogs exchanged shrugs and went back to sleep, little suspecting that their nights beside the warm fire were numbered.

*   *   *

Around noon, Bill Ellzey and I arrived at the Dixon Place, now a line camp on the Turkey Track Ranch. We unsaddled the animals and turned them out in a little trap to graze and drink from the waters of Bent's Creek, which ran right past the corrals.

All the improvements, the two-story house, the pens and barns, were built after Dixon left in the fall of 1904. We walked around for an hour looking for something that would indicate that Billy Dixon had lived here for twenty years, but we found only one trace. About fifty yards west of the corrals, eight gnarled pear trees stood in a line, all that remained of Billy's orchard. There were only two pears on these old trees and we picked them. In the shade of a giant cottonwood on the banks of the creek, we dined on jerked beef, raisins, wild currants, arrowhead lilies, and Billy's pears.

In 1972 there were still people alive who knew Billy Dixon. They remembered him as a quiet, heavy-set man who would crawl into a corner at family reunions and never open his mouth, while Jim Whippo and Cap Correll talked. When one of the children would call out, "Uncle Billy, tell us a story," he would just crawl deeper into the corner. Then Cap and Jim Whippo would trade knowing glances, and one of them would slip out of the room, returning with whiskey and glasses. When the room had begun to glow in a warm whiskey haze, the old scout would pull his chair out of the corner and tell yarn after yarn.

One of the stories Billy Dixon told has never been recorded in the history books. Back in the buffalo hunting days, he and some of his companions came upon an Indian camp on Wolf Creek in Ochiltree County. The hunters attacked the camp, laying down a deadly fire and killing everyone in sight—men, women, and children. Billy told this story only once, at a family reunion years after it happened, and before he had finshed, tears were streaming down his cheeks.

27

Until the fall of 1904, the life of Billy Dixon might have come right out of a story book. He had spent his youth taming a wild country, had retired to his ranch on the Canadian, and had fallen in love. But then tragedy struck.

Some contend that Olive wanted too much too soon and forced Billy to build her a big house at a time when he couldn't afford it. Others point to the pitiless weather of the Panhandle, the same droughts and blizzards that ruined dozens of outfits, large and small. Still others say that while Billy might have been the most competent plainsman the country ever produced, he didn't have much of a head for business. But whatever the cause, by 1904 he was losing money faster than he could make it, until only one course of action remained: to sell his holdings on Bent's Creek and move off.

It was in the fall of the year, just at the time when the Canadian valley is most beautiful. By then the first frost has nipped the cottonwood leaves and turned them a brilliant yellow. The meadow grass has gone to sleep for the winter, and the wind has stopped to rest between summer storms and winter storms. In the warm silence of early afternoon, you look out across the broad brown valley and feel that ancient sadness that people who live on the prairie feel creeping inside them in the fall—sadness that the world should be so flat and infinite, and that living things must die.

Billy saw it and felt it, and then he turned his back on the Adobe Walls ranch and walked away forever.

The family moved first to Plemons, ten miles up the river. "I lived there two years," Dixon wrote, "and found living in town worse than it could have been in jail." He still yearned for land, and every time he looked out the window he thought of his cabin on Bent's Creek. When the Oklahoma Panhandle was opened for settlement in 1906, he moved his family up to Cimarron County and filed on a quarter section. Where the country around Bent's Creek had been a veritable garden, his quarter section in Oklahoma was flat, barren, and without beauty. In the summer there was no protection from the hot scowl of the sun, and in the winter nothing to stop the howling north wind. It was a hard, stingy country. It gave nothing without a struggle and took whatever it could out of the men who worked it.

The late Woods King, Billy Dixon's nephew, told me a story once about his uncle. Back in 1913 Woods went up to

28

Oklahoma to visit the Dixons. One night when he and Uncle Billy were alone, the old scout told him, "Woods, this country's so sorry nobody can make a living on it. There's only one place for me on this earth, and that's on the Canadian River." A few weeks later he died of pneumonia. Woods King thought he was probably ready to die.

In studying the life of Billy Dixon, one perceives the sharp edge of irony appearing toward the end. For while Uncle Billy fought the Indians of the plains and contributed more than one man's share to their defeat, he understood their love for the prairies and, paradoxically, admired them deeply. His writing on the Indians appears early in *Life of Billy Dixon*:

> In savagery, a more delightful existence could not be found. What joy of physical living, with strength, health and contentment in every village . . . Of all this domain the Indian was lord and master. There was none to dispute his sway . . . His race multiplied and was happy. Food and shelter were to be found upon every hand. The white man had not come, bringing disease and poverty.

That Billy and the Indians were fighting each other is only the leading edge of the irony. The remainder lies in the fact that, in the end, both lost their land and their way of life. Those who benefited most from their struggle, the big ranchers, the railroad magnates, the town builders, were despised by both.

❂   ❂   ❂

Rested and lunched, we left the Dixon place and rode toward the Adobe Walls Battle site, a mile and a half north of the Dixon place. This was one of the most pleasant spots we had seen on the river, a broad meadow of deep luxurious grass and wildflowers in full bloom. I had seen such meadows in Vermont and upstate New York, but I had never expected to find their equal in the Texas Panhandle.

At the battle site, we left the mule and rode to a hill about half a mile to the southwest, where I had been told we would find the old Turkey Track cemetery. It lies on top of the hill, commanding a sweeping view of the whole valley. Hobbling the horses, we got down to look at the graves.

It was to this little hill that the Browns came with their son Arthur back in . . . I don't suppose anyone remembers anymore. Maybe 1890. History doesn't tell us much about the Browns, only that they had a little boy who was asleep in his bed when a rabid skunk entered the house through a hole in the screen and bit him. We found Arthur Brown's grave on the east face of the hill, a pile of white rocks marked with a piece of sandstone buried in the ground.

A few yards away, on the south face of the hill, lies another pile of stones. The wind had stolen all but a few indecipherable marks from the headstone, but I felt sure this was the spot where Billy and Olive Dixon buried an infant daughter in 1901. As I stood there over the grave, gazing off to the south to the Dixon place below, my thoughts drifted back to the beginning of the century and pieces of the story began falling in place.

Olive had carried this child inside her for nine months, had endured the pain of birth without complaint because this was pain with meaning and purpose. Maybe Grandma Walstad had come down from the flats to assist in the delivery, and having seen her work through to a successful completion, had returned home, leaving Billy with stern instructions about the care of mother and child. Everything had gone fine for several days. The old plainsman had stripped off his buckskin and donned an apron. The keen eye that had once scanned the prairies for buffalo now searched the house for signs of domestic disorder. As he mixed up a batch of biscuits in the kitchen, he smiled at the cooings of Olive and the child in the next room.

Then, suddenly, the baby died.

Olive's scream made the hair stand up on the back of his neck. He knew instinctively what it meant. He had heard her scream at tarantulas and snakes, but this was different somehow. Without stopping to wipe the sourdough from his fingers, he rushed into the next room and found her clutching the child.

A woman's grief had always baffled Billy Dixon. He had seen it many times in his life: Indian squaws clawing their breasts over the bodies of their men, pioneer women collapsing on the graves of their infants. He had never known what to say to women in sorrow, and now he didn't know what to say to Olive.

It wasn't that he was afraid of death. No, he had been close to death a dozen times, close enough to feel the Grim Reaper's icy fingers closing around his neck. At Buffalo Wallow, he and his comrades had saved back a bullet apiece for their own self-destruction in case help didn't arrive in time, before the

Comanches moved in for the last time. But then death had seemed very simple. You fought as long as you could and then you died, and if any of your comrades survived, they would grieve in silence over your remains and give you a decent burial. He could face his own death without fear, but the grief of a woman . . . that was something all his years on the plains had not prepared him for.

For five minutes he stood there, not knowing what to do. Clutching the child to her breast, Olive cursed God for allowing her baby to die, cursed Billy for bringing her to this wilderness, and then wept as though her heart would break. Billy was struck dumb by the magnitude of her grief. Like the plains or the sea or the earth itself, there seemed no end to it. Her cries filled the house and filled the valley, until it seemed the whole world had been stopped by the grief of this one tiny woman. And suddenly all the courageous resolves Billy had made about death crumbled and he knew that no mortal, not even Billy Dixon, could steel himself against the theft of life. Turning away from the bed, he rested his forehead against the wall and wept quietly.

The storm of sorrow finally spent itself. Exhausted and unable to cry another tear, Olive fell into a troubled sleep. Billy took the child from her arms, wrapped it in a clean sheet, and laid it on the bed in the other room. Later, when she awoke, he sat down beside her and tried to talk. He wanted to talk of God and the meaning of life, but he ended up telling her there was a dead child in the house and they would have to start thinking about a burial. His plain, blunt way of putting it shocked her at first, but by then she was ready to draw on the strength a man brings to such occasions. Mist came to her eyes as she thought of leaving her baby girl alone on the prairie.

He knew what she was thinking. "Honey," he said, patting her hand, "we'll bury her up on the hill. That way she can always see a light in our window when it gets dark."

She nodded. "All right. But, Billy, don't dig the grave too deep. It's so cold in the winter!"

The next day he took his little girl up to the cemetery on the hill. As Olive had requested, he dug a shallow grave. But he knew the wolves and coyotes would find the grave and dig it up, so he spent the whole day carrying rocks up the hill and placing them over the fresh earth. It was hard work, but when he had finished, he stepped back from the grave and felt that he had done something for his girl.

31

When he got back to the house, he took Olive to the window and pointed to the mound of rocks on top of the hill. "There she is, Olive. Our little girl's not lost. She's right there, and every time you look out the window, you'll know she's still with us."

✿ ✿ ✿

Dobbin, whom we had left tied down at Adobe Walls, was raising a ruckus by this time, bellowing to the horses in that peculiar, indescribable bray of his. It wasn't a hee-haw or a whinny, but a disoriented kind of sound, both inarticulate and yet very expressive of a mule's loneliness. So we rode back down to the Walls and assured our mule that he was still loved and wanted. He seemed very glad to see the horses, and as usual, regarded Bill and me as intruders.

V

The Battle of Adobe Walls

In 1867 President Andrew Johnson appointed a peace commission to meet with the five major tribes of Plains Indians and to reach an accord with them. Among those he appointed were Generals Sherman and Harney, Indian Commissioner Nathaniel Taylor, and other senators and dignitaries. In October they arrived at Medicine Lodge, Kansas, to meet with a delegation of chiefs headed by Satanta, Kicking Bird, and Lone Wolf of the Kiowas; Black Kettle and White Antelope of the Cheyennes; and Little Raven of the Arapahoes. Also present at this historic occasion were Henry Stanley of the *New York Tribune* (four years later Stanley would journey to Africa to find David Livingstone), William F. Cody (also known to us as Buffalo Bill), and Billy Dixon, then a government teamster.

For a whole week before the actual council began, each side worked at allaying the suspicions of the other. The soldiers kept an open house under a grove of trees, where they offered coffee, sugar, and soda crackers to the Indians, and distributed such articles as saddles, blankets, and blue overalls. The Indians responded by inviting their white brothers to a huge feast, where a hundred dogs were basted and barbecued and served by Indian butlers wearing blue overalls.

But these shows of friendship and generosity merely glossed over the differences between the two worlds. The commission from Washington had come prepared to be generous with its

Beneath this forlorn sandstone grave marker lie the remains of Arthur Brown, a child who died from the bite of a rabid skunk before the turn of the century. The grave is located in the old Turkey Track cemetery which overlooks the Adobe Walls battle site.

overalls but with little else. From the government's point of view, the purpose of the Council was to induce the Indians to retire to reservations where, it was hoped, they would become thrifty farmers and solid citizens. The commission had come to Medicine Lodge to sign a treaty, and sign they did. It called for the Indians to retire to reservation lands, cease their depredations, and allow the railroads to build through their land. In return for these concessions, they were to be issued annuity goods, and all the land south of the Arkansas River was declared off limits to white hunters.

Why either side bothered to sign the treaty is a mystery, since time proved neither overly scrupulous in abiding by its provisions. The treaty was worthless from the very beginning. In the first place, it is doubtful that the Indians even understood what they were signing. The official interpreter for the council, Phillip McCusker, spoke only Comanche, while the spokesmen for the Indians were Kiowas and Cheyennes. One can imagine that by the time legal English had been translated through two or three Indian dialects, the message had become somewhat garbled. In the second place, the Indians who signed the paper had no authority to enforce such an agreement because such authority did not exist in their culture. They had no congress, no courts of law, no social or legal structures that would have given a chief the right to force his young braves to observe the treaty. And finally, a hundred years of treaty-making had left the Indians with little respect for legal agreements. Most had come to Medicine Lodge strictly for a good time and free food. For that they would have signed a dozen treaties, and a dozen treaties wouldn't have changed their behavior any more than one did.

And while the whites entered into the treaty with an outward show of gravity, one doubts that they ever intended to keep the buffalo hunters north of the Arkansas. The government, which considered the wild Indians a bur in the flesh of progress, realized that the economy of the Plains tribes depended on an abundant supply of buffalo. Extending the logic one step, they understood that when the buffalo disappeared, so would the wild Indians.

The treaty was doomed to failure, and it doesn't even matter which side broke it first.

In 1871 when the construction of the Santa Fe Railroad stopped at Granada, Colorado, hundreds of men were thrown out of work and had to find another way of making a living. Some left the country, but many turned to buffalo hunting. In the winter of 1872–73 the country was full of hunters and the buffalo fell in record numbers. The number of buffalo north of the Arkansas River decreased rapidly until almost none remained, and gradually the hunters began slipping across the river into the Indian hunting grounds.

Among them was Billy Dixon, who had witnessed the signing of the Medicine Lodge Treaty and knew that hunting south of the river was a violation of the treaty. His attitude was probably typical. He intended to hunt south of the Arkansas until someone stopped him. In March of 1874 he met with a group of hunters and merchants in Dodge City. After discussing the dwindling supply of buffalo north of the Arkansas, they decided to drift south in the spring and set up a hunting camp on the Canadian River in the Texas Panhandle.

The party established a camp on Bent's Creek near the site of Adobe Walls, an old trading post built by Colonel William Bent in the 1840s and abandoned a few years later. At this permanent camp, Myers and Leonard established a small store, James Hanrahan built a saloon, and Thomas O'Keefe added a blacksmith shop—all of sod and picket construction. When the buffalo came through on their summer migration north, the hunters worked out of temporary camps within a radius of twenty or thirty miles of Adobe Walls and returned every week or so to exchange hides for ammunition and supplies.

The hunting went well for several weeks. Then, in June, word reached the Walls that two hunters named Dudley and Wallace had been killed by Indians on Chicken Creek, some twenty-five miles downriver. A few days later it was reported that two more hunters had fallen under the scalping knife on Salt Fork of the Red. At Adobe Walls, on the sultry night of June 25, twenty-eight men and one woman sat around in small groups discussing the Indian situation. The threat seemed to have come and gone, and the hunters talked of returning to their hunting camps the following morning.

Over in Indian Territory, the Comanches, Kiowas, and Cheyennes were seething with bitterness and desperation. Their backs had not been completely broken, but the old ways were rapidly slipping away. Something had gone wrong. Their power had failed them, and unless something happened quickly the old ways would be lost forever. On all sides they began looking for a sign, a prophet, a new power that would enable them to drive the white man out of the country.

It was then that a young and untested medicine man appeared on the scene. There wasn't much poetry in his name—Coyote Droppings (Ishatai)—but he gave evidence of having strong power. Not only did he claim to have spoken with the Great Spirit, but he was said to be immune to bullets. When he belched up a wagonload of cartridges and swallowed them again in the presence of witnesses, word spread that the Comanches had found their messiah. At the annual Sun Dance that spring of 1874, Ishatai exhorted his people to go to war against the white man. If they didn't fight now, he said, the buffalo would be exterminated and the Indians would fall to the level of the lowly Caddos and other reservation tribes. Some of the Indians found Ishatai's sermons a bit too strong and quietly slipped out of the Sun Dance camp. But many Kiowas, Arapahoes, Comanches, and Cheyennes were ready to follow him on the war trail.

One of these was a young Noconi Comanche war chief named Quanah Parker. The half-breed son of Chief Peta Nocona and Cynthia Ann Parker, a white captive of the Comanches, Quanah carried a bitter hatred for the white man. In 1860 a party of soldiers from Ft. Belknap, Texas, had virtually exterminated his Noconi band, killing his father and taking his mother prisoner. More recently, his favorite cousin had been killed on a raid into Texas, and Quanah had been waiting for a chance to avenge his death. So when Ishatai had gotten the Indians talking about war, Quanah went from village to village with his pipe. As was customary, he was crying for the unavenged cousin. "My cousin was killed," he lamented in each village, "and his bones are still in Texas. I want revenge. I want you to take my pipe." When Ishatai was consulted, he affirmed that this would be a good raid.

Between them, Quanah and the medicine man were able to gather seven hundred Kiowas, Cheyennes, Arapahoes, and Comanches. The night before their departure, several warrior societies held a big dance near the head of the Washita River in the Panhandle. The next morning Quanah dispatched seven scouts to the Canadian River. The following day they returned and reported finding the hunters at Adobe Walls, and the Indians rode off to make war.

That evening before sundown they stopped, unsaddled their horses, painted their faces, and made medicine. At dusk they

37

moved across the Canadian in fours and then walked their horses up Adobe Creek. Just before dawn the order was given to mount up. The warriors formed a long line and charged just as the sun was coming up.

The night before, the hunters had bedded down outside the buildings at Adobe Walls. The feeling in camp that evening had been one of security and celebration, to the point of sheer carelessness. No one had suspected the Indians were in the country, and the hunters didn't even bother posting a guard for the night. But for one fateful accident, the Indians might have galloped into the camp and slaughtered the hunters in their beds.

The accident happened around two in the morning. All at once the camp was awakened by what sounded like a rifle shot. In an instant the men sprang out of their beds and had their weapons ready to return the fire. Then a sleepy voice inside Hanrahan's Saloon called off the alarm, saying the sound had come from a broken ridge pole in the roof. (In later years Billy Dixon would look upon this accident as the work of Providence.) About fifteen men got up and repaired the ridge pole, as there was some danger of the whole roof collapsing if it were not replaced at once. By the time another pole had been cut and put into place, the sky was red with dawn and the men decided to stay up and get an early start out to the buffalo range. As Dixon was rolling up his bedding, he looked off to the east and saw something moving in the distance. In the half-darkness he couldn't make out what it was. Then he heard the thunder of hooves and the "hideous cries" of seven hundred Indians.

There was never a more splendidly barbaric sight. In after years I was glad that I had seen it. Hundreds of warriors, the flower of the fighting men of the southwestern Plains tribes, mounted upon their finest horses, armed with guns and lances, and carrying heavy shields of thick buffalo hide, were coming like the wind. Over all was splashed the rich colors of red, vermillion, and ochre, on the bodies of the men, on the bodies of the running horses. Scalps dangled from bridles, gorgeous war-bonnets fluttered their plumes, bright feathers dangled from the tails and manes of the horses, and the bronzed, half-naked bodies of the riders glittered with ornaments of silver and brass.

38

Dixon seized his gun, fired off a few shots, and made a dash for Hanrahan's Saloon. Half-dressed men stumbled out of their beds and ran for cover, as bullets zinged through the still morning air and thocked into the sod walls.

In this first charge the Indians made their only scores of the day. The Shadler brothers, sleeping in a wagon with their big Newfoundland dog, did not hear the alarm. All three, the brothers and the dog, were killed and scalped. Billy Tyler was shot down as he ran toward Myers and Leonard's store. Also killed in the charge were fifty-six horses and twenty-eight head of oxen.

Once the hunters had barricaded themselves in the buildings, they began returning the fire with large bore Sharps and Springfield rifles. The Indians, believing themselves immune to bullets as a result of Ishatai's medicine, charged again and again into the range of the big guns, each time sustaining heavier losses than they could inflict. By noon they abandoned this tactic and withdrew to the red hills east of the Walls, where they continued sniping into the buildings.

Now the battle lapsed into a war of nerves. The Indians stationed themselves around the hills, just out of range, and waited. That night the hunters slept little and kept their guns at the ready. The next day the Indians were still there. On the third day a party of about fifteen Indians appeared on a bluff east of Adobe Creek. With nothing better to do, Dixon decided to take a shot at one of them with his big Sharps .50. He adjusted the sights, took careful aim, and fired. The Indian toppled off his horse and fell to the ground. The distance was later paced off at 1538 yards, seven-eighths of a mile. This was probably the most celebrated single shot ever fired in the Indian wars, though Dixon later admitted that it had been a "scratch shot." But it had the right effect on the Indians. Dispirited and angry at Ishatai's "polecat medicine," they rode away.

Having lost only thirteen dead, the Indians hadn't suffered a serious defeat, but the battle had dealt them a terrible psychological blow. It had proved that they had lost the medicine that had made them lords for two centuries. In July, Washington launched a four-pronged offensive against the Indians, and by the time the first snows fell they were a defeated people, housed in concentration camps along Cache Creek near Ft. Sill.[1]

* * *

Today there is nothing left to see at Adobe Walls but a collection of stone markers, one honoring the buffalo hunters and another erected by an Indian historical society to honor its heroes. In a way, the presence of these two monuments is symbolic of the confusion that has crept into our view of frontier history in recent years. We can see that both sides had their reasons for fighting and that both fought bravely, but when questions of value and judgement arise, we are hard pressed for answers. History tells us who won, but nobody seems really sure any more who *should* have won. Indeed, some modern writers seem to be saying that the Indians should have won, that they were the wronged party, and that if they had won we would have been spared the curse of modern civilization and its discontents.

I remember reading an article in the July 2, 1971 issue of *Life* magazine, in which an Indian specialist, presumably white, analyzed the expansion of Anglo-American civilization in terms of "land greed" and "Christian ethnocentrism." This struck me as rather ungrateful, especially since it appeared in one of America's best known magazines. That Time-Life had profited immensely from Christian ethnocentrism and land greed, that their sky-scraper in New York City stood on a piece of land the Dutch swindled from the Manhatte Indians had apparently been forgotten.

I also wondered at the relevance of the author's point. Was he suggesting that Indians such as the Comanches and Kiowas were *not* land-greedy and ethnocentric? I had always understood that the Kiowas and Comanches got their land the same way we did—they stole it, by murder and brute force, from the Mescaleros, Lipans, Tonkawas, Caddos, Pueblos, Jumanos, Spaniards, French, and Mexicans.

So who were the heroes of the Battle of Adobe Walls: Quanah and Ishatai, or Billy Dixon and Bat Masterson? We can find examples of land greed, ethnocentrism, and cruelty on both sides; also tenderness, heroism, and courage. But if we can no longer celebrate our victory over the Indians and applaud the efforts of men such as Billy Dixon, then maybe we can do the next best thing and quietly appreciate the fruits of their struggle, knowing that when pressed we're not about to give the country back to the Indians, heroes or no heroes. In the end, maybe this is the best way of putting the Indian wars into perspective. If Satanta and Quanah and Dohasan had won, we would have been spared the grief of Viet Nam, racial strife, pollution, high taxes, the hydrogen bomb, drugs, and a generation of children that keeps reminding us of our failures. We would have been spared a lot of things, because we wouldn't be here —and I doubt very much that our Indian brothers would be grieving.

Second night's camp on the Turkey Track Ranch.

VI

Cutting for Sign

By the time we crossed Adobe Creek the shadows were about five o'clock long and the tyranny of the midday sun had lessened a bit. We probably should have made camp on the creek, but we hadn't traveled much that day and were anxious to push on down the river. And after all, for the past two days we had seen ideal camping spots everywhere we looked, so there was no reason to think the country would change all of a sudden.

The country changed all of a sudden. On crossing Adobe Creek, we left the lush green meadows behind and found ourselves in a harsh forbidding country of high sand hills, thinly grassed and dotted with soapweed and skunkbrush. An hour passed as we looked in vain for possible camp sites. We didn't even see a tree in this country, much less a spring of water. Our expectations declined by the minute until we resolved to stop at the first windmill we came to. But looking around in a circle, we saw no sign of a windmill, only mile upon mile of sand hills. Finally we split up. I rode south to scout the country from the tops of the hills, while Bill and the mule moved on in an easterly direction. Eventually we both sighted a windmill in the distance and rode toward it.

We made camp near an old cottonwood tree about three hundred yards from the windmill, reasoning that it would be easier to transport water than firewood. Within thirty minutes we had hobbled the horses, pitched and trenched the tent, doctored cuts and sores on the animals, and had water boiling over a big cottonwood fire. We dined that night on rice with bouillon, fried bacon, gravy, and dried fruit, and darkness found us inside the tent, jotting down notes by lantern light and swigging hot sassafras tea.

The next morning Bill gathered up our waterbags and canteens and went down to the windmill for water. It was then that I discovered I had lost my canteen in the sand hills the previous afternoon. I despaired of ever finding it again.

While Bill was gone, I looked up from the cooking fire and spotted a terrapin crawling through the sand nearby. I had heard old-timers tell of Plains Indians gathering hundreds of these turtles and baking them in the coals of a campfire, but I had never known anyone who had actually eaten baked terrapin, or who could offer a reliable opinion on it one way or another. So I decided to try it myself. By the time Bill returned with the water, I had cracked open the shell and was taking my first bite of baked land turtle. He glanced at the shell in my hand and curled his lip. Between bites, I tried to explain that it was the responsibility of the younger generation to preserve these old recipes and pass them on to the yet-unborn. He nodded, filled his plate with rice and raisins, and retired to another part of the camp.

For the benefit of the next generation, here is my informed opinion of baked terrapin. After baking it for twenty minutes, you crack open the under side of the shell and marvel at all the luscious meat that isn't there. And then you understand why the Indians gathered *hundreds* of them. The best protection the terrapin has against a hungry race of men is not his shell, but rather the fact that the shell is practically empty. The terrapin, which looks so plump crawling over the prairie, is composed of entrails, legs, and a lot of empty space. What meat you find isn't bad, a strip of white around the neck which has a fishy taste, and the dark meat of the legs which resembles cottontail rabbit. But I think maybe the best advice I could pass on to the generations unborn is to put baked terrapin, along with jackrabbit and prickly pear, at the bottom of the list of interesting foods.

After breakfast we sand-washed the pans and broke down the camp. Looking out at the sand hills in front of us, I began to fret about my lost canteen, at which time Bill wondered why

I didn't pick up my trail of yesterday afternoon and backtrack until I found it. Why indeed. I cinched up Dollarbill and rode back to the windmill, confident that I would find neither trail nor canteen.

The procedure one follows in locating a trail is called "cutting for sign." Essentially, you ride in a wide circle until you cross the trail. Cutting for sign is not something people do much anymore. I first encountered the expression in Mr. Haley's biography of Charles Goodnight, which I began reading one afternoon in my grandfather's library in Seminole. That was the day I discovered the checkmark Grampy Buck had left in the margin on page forty-nine, beside the paragraph that began, "On their way out to the open country [the Indians] came to where a man by the name of Sherman had settled on Stagg Prairie, in the western edge of Parker County." At the bottom of the page, I read of the death of Mrs. Ezra Sherman, my grandmother's grandmother.

This was in the fall of 1860, when the settlements in Parker, Palo Pinto, and Jack Counties constituted the westernmost thrust of civilization. Theoretically, the Indian problem had been solved in 1858 when the state of Texas had moved all its Indians across the Red River into what is now Oklahoma. But this did not stop the Comanches. They came and went at their leisure, killed and raped whom they pleased, and rode back across the Red River loaded down with the spoils of war. By the fall of 1860, the whole Brazos country was ablaze, the citizenry close to panic. People were saying that the Comanches intended to ride into Weatherford on Christmas day and take over the whole town, and few doubted they could do it.

Sam Houston was governor at this time and had followed the events on the frontier with concern. But The Raven, like so many of the men who had met the Indians face-to-face, had a warm spot in his heart for the savages and considered himself their friend. But of course he had never known any Comanches, only the civilized tribes to the south to whose lodges he had often fled to smoke and talk away his doubts about civilization. Houston resisted the instincts of his time and culture, when the extermination of the Indians was not a grotesque idea, but something most Texans accepted as necessary and good. The pity is that he chose the Comanches as the object of his humanism, for if there was ever a race of people on earth that could prove humanism untenable, it was the Comanches. They did

45

not understand his idealism and had no use for the peace he wanted.

When he could no longer ignore the reports from the frontier, he dispatched Colonel M. T. Johnson to the Brazos country with vague orders to punish the warring Indians wherever he found them. Colonel Johnson and his men spent several months scouting the gambling halls and whiskey mills around Ft. Belknap, but did little about the Indians.

Then, in November, a band of Noconi Comanches under Chief Peta Nocona slipped into Lost Valley northwest of Weatherford. At John Brown's ranch they stopped to pay their respects to the owner—scalped him, cut off his nose, lanced his body full of holes, and stole his horses. From there they rode to the Sherman place on Rock Creek. Finding Mrs. Sherman alone with two small children, unarmed, and pregnant, they tied her to the ground, raped her repeatedly, ripped the long auburn hair from her skull, and shot three arrows into her body. Somehow she managed to survive for two days, long enough to relate the grisly story to horrified neighbors. The story flashed across the whole frontier, from Ft. Griffin to Clarksville, and in a matter of weeks the outraged citizenry united in a cry for revenge—a cry that Sam Houston heard loud and clear.

On December 12, 1860, the *Dallas Herald* carried this impassioned letter:

> Need we reiterate to you the heart-rending narratives disclosed by Mrs. Sherman, who, thank God, survived long enough with the sense God gave her, to tell much of the brutal and fiendish treatment she received at their hands?
>
> Do you see fifty-five Red Demons seize upon her trembling form, drag her away into an open prairie, and abuse her person with damning violence, too revolting to be known in a Christian world?
>
> Now one winds her beautiful and flowing hair around his left hand, with his right inserts the scalping knife, entirely around her head, just above the ears, places his right foot upon the neck of her prostrate body, and while the suffering and innocent woman shrieks and cries for mercy, he tears away the covering of nature, leaving the skull bone bare!

Today it is hard for us to take seriously anyone who writes of "heart-rending narratives" and "Red Demons." But this kind of language appeared in newspapers, petitions, and letters from

46

one end of the frontier to the other, and Governor Houston took it seriously, dispatching Sul Ross, the new captain of the Texas Rangers, to Ft. Belknap with orders to draw blood. On December 13 Ross's Rangers were joined by twenty-three dragoons from Camp Cooper and seventy volunteers from Parker and Jack Counties, and the force marched north toward the Pease River. At the head of the column rode Charles Goodnight, at twenty-four already the best scout in the region.

Several days later the trail of the Indians disappeared into a large herd of buffalo. This was no accident. Although the Comanches had never been pursued into the sanctuaries along the Red and Pease Rivers, they had ridden into the buffalo to confuse anyone who might be following them. Goodnight may have been confused for a moment, but he simply rode to the other side of the herd, cut for sign, and picked up the trail again. On the eighteenth, he spotted a book lying on the ground, where it had been dropped by the Indians. Getting down to investigate, he discovered it to be Mrs. Sherman's Bible, which the Comanches had taken to use as packing in their war shields. Just a few minutes after he had picked up the Bible, Goodnight located the Indian camp on the south side of the Pease River.

The Battle of Pease River didn't last more than a few minutes. The Comanches were taken completely by surprise, most of them cut down before they could string an arrow or reach their horses. Only two Indians escaped death that day. One was the green-eyed squaw of Peta Nocona, a white captive who had lived among the Comanches for twenty-five years. She was taken prisoner by Sul Ross and eventually returned to her family in East Texas. Her name, of course, was Cynthia Ann Parker. The other who escaped death that day was Cynthia's twelve-year-old son, a boy named Quanah, who fourteen years later would lead the raid on Adobe Walls.[1]

One hot afternoon in the summer of 1969, I drove to Weatherford, Texas, to talk with a man named Fred Cotten, the unofficial historian of Parker County. I had seen his name in the Parker County file in the Texas Archives library in Austin, and had driven to Weatherford in hopes he could direct me to the grave of great-great-Grandmother Sherman.

I found him in his place of business on Oak Street, across from the old stone courthouse. In this large building on the square, he operated a furniture store on the north and a funeral parlor on the south, with an open door between the two.

47

Though well up in years, he was a handsome gentleman with a shock of white hair and a pair of penetrating brown eyes. He struck me at first glance as a man who had found a nice balance between small town respectability and the stubborn individualism of another era. He presided over his fortress of probity and commerce in a pair of baggy pants strung up with white suspenders, a wrinkled shirt, and a token four-in-hand tie that hung loose at his open collar.

At the rear of the furniture store, I told Mr. Cotten my name and offered my hand. When I mentioned that I was a descendant of Mrs. Sherman, he seemed pleased. We went to the front of the store, seated ourselves on one of his display couches, and talked under the whisper of the overhead fans.

Yes, he knew where Mrs. Sherman was buried because he had located her unmarked grave in Willow Springs Cemetery and placed a granite tombstone there at his own expense. It seems he had always been interested in the Sherman episode and was touched by her dying request to be buried at Willow Springs near a church. As he gave me directions to the cemetery, the bell on the funeral parlor door jingled and two ladies walked in. He stood up, dismissed me, and went off to take care of his customers.

From Weatherford I drove east on the busy Ft. Worth highway until I came to Willow Springs Cemetery, which owes its very existence in the present day to Fred Cotten. A few years back, when the state shot lines for a new four-lane highway between Weatherford and Ft. Worth, it appeared that it would pass right through the middle of Willow Springs Cemetery. The engineers pointed out that it would cost the taxpayers so many thousands of dollars to put a curve in the road. Fred Cotten pointed out that he didn't give a damn how much it cost, they had better stay out of Willow Springs Cemetery or he'd sell everything he had and keep them in court for five years.

Today highway 180 between Weatherford and Ft. Worth goes right past the entrance of Willow Springs Cemetery, and in the cemetery is a gravestone which reads,

Martha Sherman
Killed by Indians in 1860
Buried at Willow Springs to be near a church

✿   ✿   ✿

But anyway, on the morning of June 21, 1972, I had lost my canteen and found myself practicing the forgotten art of cutting for sign in the Canadian River valley. After cutting several arcs just west of the windmill, I located the trail and followed it toward the sand hills. I had gone into this maneuver grimly fatalistic, and it came as quite a shock when, a hundred yards beyond the windmill, I discovered my lost canteen.

VII

John's Creek Rodeo

From the windmill camp we rode east, skirting a low line of bluffs on the north side of the river. Around noon we reached John's Creek, the first live water we had seen since leaving Bent's Creek fifteen miles upriver. Here we swung north and followed the creek a mile and a half until we came to a cottonwood grove with a nice sandy beach on the creek nearby. Spreading the tarp in the shade, we unsaddled the animals and put them out to graze, and then we sat down to do a little grazing of our own, on our standard lunch ration of jerky and raisins. After lunch, we hustled down to the creek, stripped down to hair and skin, and plunged into the waters of John's Creek, which must have been every bit of four inches deep. We would have preferred a swim but settled for a bath instead. I lay down in the middle of the creek and parted the waters with my head, surrendering my body to the tickle of passing minnows and water striders, while a few yards upstream my partner washed himself as methodically as a cat. It was very peaceful lying there in the water and listening to the gobble of wild turkeys in the distance.

About an hour later, refreshed and ready for a calm unhurried ride to Ed Brainard's place, we climbed on our horses and headed east. When we came to a pasture gate, I got down to open it since Bill had the mule in tow. Just as I had gotten back into the saddle, Dobbin the mule spooked at something,

50

exactly what we shall never know. He took a few little hop steps forward and then began to buck. In the process he got the halter rope fouled around Suds's hindquarters, and an instant later Suds had joined the rodeo.

All at once, Bill was in a bad position. In his left hand he held the reins of a bucking horse—and Suds wasn't just humping up his back; he was *bucking*—and in his right hand, the halter rope of a bucking mule. He might have been able to ride out one or the other, but with both animals working on him at the same time, he was doomed. Dobbin bucked south and Suds bucked north, and, still hanging on, Bill split the difference between them. I saw the trouble and tried to ride into the fray to take the mule, but Dollarbill began to pitch and I had my own problems to worry about.

Bill held on valiantly but Suds finally bedded him down, took the reins away from him, and bucked a complete circle around us. On every jump Bill's four hundred dollar Nikon camera, which he had dallied around the horn, crashed against the saddle. The higher Suds bucked the harder the camera struck the saddle, and the harder the camera smacked the saddle the higher he bucked. As Suds came back around to the point at which he had started bucking, Dobbin stampeded again, demanding Bill's full attention. Bill dug his heels into the ground and took a double grip on the rope. In stubbornness, he was Dobbin's equal any day, but the mule enjoyed a weight advantage of some five hundred pounds, and with a toss of his head he managed to jerk Bill out of the trenches his heels had dug in the sand, and off they went across the pasture. Bill ran as hard and fast as he could—too fast, in fact, as he took his second spill of the day. In a scramble of arms and legs, he flew, bareback, into a clump of sagebrush.

In almost the same instant, the camera flew off Suds's saddle, sailed ten feet through the air, and crashed to the ground.

And then Dobbin went to work bucking at the pack saddle, and at any moment I expected to see a blizzard of pots, pans, plates, jerky, raisins, and rice in the Texas sky. I held my breath and waited. Dobbin took five jumps and gave up. The load remained on his back.

It had been a wreck, but not such a bad one. Bill checked out his camera and found, to his astonishment, that it still functioned. Bill himself had the imprint of a sagebrush on his back, but otherwise had come through in good shape. He caught

Suds, held a private conference with him on the subject of future rodeos, and climbed back in the saddle. I will always admire Bill for that. In the years since we made our trip, I have been unloaded by a few horses that were young and stout, as Suds was, and I know that it takes courage to get back on. Bill climbed back on and rode him, and Suds never bucked again.

Until three days later.

VIII

John's Creek Tales

The Brainard family had been on the river since the very beginning. The old man E. H. Brainard came to the Panhandle in 1882 to cowboy for the old Bar CC Ranch, which at that time controlled some fourteen hundred square miles of land in Roberts and Ochiltree Counties. E. H. Brainard was assigned to work out of the John's Creek line camp at the western edge of the ranch, where he lived in a three-room frame house. When the Bar CC pulled out of the Panhandle, ruined by the blizzard of 1886 which wiped out seventy percent of its cattle, Brainard filed on three sections of land around John's Creek and began working to put his own ranch together. Ninety years later, the ranch was being operated by his son, Bud Brainard, and grandsons Ed Brainard and Ben McIntyre.

We arrived at the Ed Brainard place around five in the afternoon. After consuming what seemed gallons of iced tea, we followed Ed down to the corral to take care of the animals. We had originally planned to stop briefly at the house, then ride on down to Willow Creek to make our camp for the night, but Ed and his wife Lilith had dismissed this idea as preposterous, saying they had an empty trailer house nearby and we might as well use it. We accepted the offer. Down at the corral, we stowed our gear in the saddlehouse, while Ed fed the animals hay and oats and doctored Dobbin's cinch sore with salty meat grease, an old-timey wound dressing.

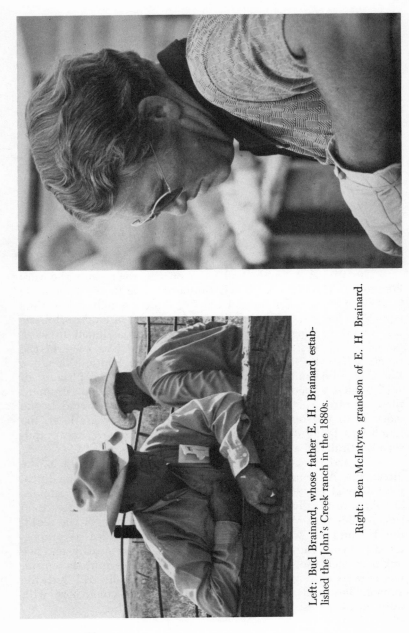

Left: Bud Brainard, whose father E. H. Brainard established the John's Creek ranch in the 1880s.

Right: Ben McIntyre, grandson of E. H. Brainard.

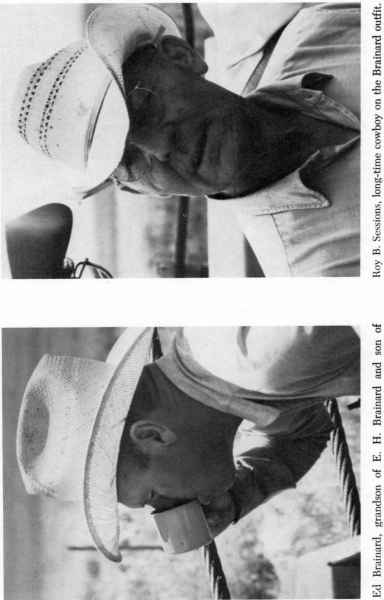

Ed Brainard, grandson of E. H. Brainard and son of Bud Brainard.

Roy B. Sessions, long-time cowboy on the Brainard outfit.

When we arrived at the trailer, we found it in a state of activity, as the four Brainard girls, Berklee, Amy, Sally, and little blue-eyed Sena, rushed around dusting, picking up, making beds, and putting things in order. Berklee even left us with a vase of wildflowers.

An hour later, we took our seats around the long plank table in the Brainard dining room and helped ourselves to generous portions of ham, beef tips in gravy, mashed potatoes, green salad, fresh biscuits, and homemade grape jelly. When Lilith had the audacity to apologize for the meal, we rolled our eyes and reminded her that we had been dining on jerked beef and rice for the past three days—though from the amount of food we put away, she might have suspected grub worms and cactus spines.

During the meal I sat across the table from little Sena, whose sky blue eyes and cherubic face captured my attention. I was fascinated that a child born in the age of space travel should be identified with a name as old as Sena. In two or three years she would start the first grade, taking her place among a host of Tammys and Tinas, Sherrys and Cindys, and she would be the only Sena in school.

She was named after Sena Walstad King, one of seven daughters of C. J. and Marion Walstad, who lived on the flats north of the river in Ochiltree County. Since there were no boys to help Father Walstad look after his cattle on the open range, Sena was taught to ride and rope at an early age. One summer day in 1887, while riding up Picket Canyon, she saw a half-grown bear lumbering through the brush ahead of her. Most girls—and boys too—would have left the scene in a hurry, but not Sena Walstad. Calmly she took the rope from her saddle, coaxed her frightened horse into range, roped the bear, dragged it home, and made a pet of it.[1]

A few years later she married Archie King, another Bar CC cowboy, and they moved into the John's Creek camp with E. H. Brainard. In 1892 she gave birth to a son not fifty feet from where little Sena Brainard and I were eating our supper. His name was Woods King, and he probably knew more about the Canadian River country and its history than any man of his generation. I was very fortunate to have spent many hours with Mr. King, asking questions, checking dates and names and historical sites. At the age of eighty, he still had a wonderful memory and a dry sense of humor. He died at the age of eighty-

56

one in June of 1973—exactly a year after I ate supper in the house where he was born, across the table from the little girl who was named for his mother.

When plates had been shined with biscuit mops and chairs pushed back from the table, we settled into some good yarn swapping. Bill told the story of his rodeo down by John's Creek that afternoon, and Ed howled and cackled. He understood. He'd broken a leg in a similar experience two years before.

Any storytelling session on the Brainard ranch leads inevitably to Jim Scolfield. Jim, a tall strong man who feared nothing and nobody, worked as a cowboy and wolfer for the old man Brainard back in the 1890s, and for years after. When he was wolfing, Jim's job was to hunt down and kill loafer wolves that were a scourge to the cattlemen back in the early days. These animals, extinct today except in the northern states, were both larger and more destructive than their coyote cousins, for while a coyote could satisfy himself on carrion, the wolves preferred a fresh kill at every meal. Working in pairs or packs, they would run a weak calf or even a full grown cow, slashing at the hind legs until the tendons had been severed.

Some wolfers used dogs or traps, but not Jim Scolfield. In the spring, when the loafer pups arrived, he would ride horseback until he spotted a she-wolf trotting across the plains. Then he would follow her to her den. His *modus operandi* from this point was very simple: since the wolves wouldn't come out to him, he went in after them. Preceded by his six-shooter, he would snake his shoulders through the narrow hole until he had reached a point where he could see their eyes glowing in the gloom. Then he would open fire on the mother and drag the pups from the den.

Wolves usually chose the rocky ledges around the canyons for their dens, but one time Jim followed a wolf to a hole in a sandy bank. Tying his horse to a plum thicket, he loaded his pistol and started into the hole. He inched and wiggled his way into the narrow passage until only his boots remained outside. Then, with just enough light sifting through the hole to illuminate the yellow eyes of the mother wolf, he raised his pistol and took aim, just as he had done many times before. But before he could pull off a shot, the sand above him collapsed, cutting off his escape—and even worse, snuffing out the light.

And there was Big Jim, locked in a dark tomb with a lobo wolf.

As the shadows stretched out across the Canadian valley that evening, Mr. Brainard noticed Jim's absence and began to worry. Fearing his wolfer had met with an accident, he rode out across the country and eventually located Jim's horse, still tied to the plum thicket. He rode in a big circle around the horse and called out, but no one answered. When darkness fell, he abandoned the search and rode back to the ranchhouse, puzzled and worried over what could have happened to Jim.

The next morning he organized his cowboys into a search party and returned to the plum thicket. "Boys," he said, "Jim's horse was tied to this thicket, so he couldn't be very far away. I want you to get down on your hands and knees and search every inch of ground until we find him." And that's what they did, beginning in a tight circle and moving outward, until one of the men spotted a boot heel protruding from the sand.

They dug him out and he was still alive. I wish we had a record of what he said.

Scolfield also saw action during the brief range war of the 1890s. At that time a number of settlers came to the river country looking for land and a fresh start. The big ranchers, who had been on the river for ten and fifteen years, resented the intrusion of these "nesters," while the nesters were jealous of the influence of the large outfits. Squabbling arose over fences, water rights, timber, and political issues, and both sides armed for a fight. Haystacks on the Brainard and Turkey Track Ranches were burned, and cattle were gut-shot with small caliber rifles, so that the animals would live for several days and then die when the sniper was far away.

Jim Scolfield often went out on horseback for days at a time, observing with field glasses the burning and shooting. He knew everyone involved, and the other faction had let it be known that they intended to run E. H. Brainard out of the country and kill Scolfield. They did not succeed in doing either. Captain Bill McDonald of the Texas Rangers entered the case, and the Panhandle Range War ended with no major bloodshed.[2]

Years later, Jim suffered a stroke that put an end to his career as a cowboy. Too crippled to ride a horse any more, he moved down to Canadian where he raised vegetables on a little patch of land Mr. Brainard had given him. He made enough to live on, with a little left over for entertainment.

One day he hobbled into a saloon on Main Street in Canadian to have a little snort. Inside, he got to talking with another man, and by the middle of the afternoon both were well oiled. No doubt they had started out swapping horse and cowboy stories from the old days, laughing at jokes and giving each other a good-natured ribbing. But as the afternoon progressed, the whiskey began to talk and the humor went sour, until they were flinging insults at each other with no pretense of fun. Then the other fellow made a serious mistake. He called Jim an uncomplimentary name.

In his prime, Jim would have invited the man outside, or more likely, thrashed him on the spot while the insult was still fresh in both their minds. But now he suffered the double humiliation of old age: not only was he worthless as a cowboy, but he cut such a pathetic figure that no one would fight him. He wouldn't have minded taking a whipping, but the fact that the other man wouldn't even give him a chance to defend his honor was intolerable. Without a word, he left the bar and went home to "get the difference": the old six-shooter he had carried into wolf dens and packed during the range war. He hobbled back to town and waited for the scoundrel to emerge. When he did, Jim took careful aim and squeezed the trigger. Struck in the chest, the man fell to the ground.

Having performed the awful deed, Jim didn't know what to do next. He didn't intend to run; Jim Scolfield had never run from anything or anybody in his life. But neither did he want to turn himself in to the sheriff. So, unable to think of anything better, he went to consult the best friend he had in the world, E. H. Brainard.

Mr. Brainard had just eased into a nice hot tub of water and was looking forward to a peaceful bath when he heard a tap at the door, and in walked Jim, stone-faced and pale. "Mr. Brainard, I just shot a man on Main Street. What do you reckon I ought to do?"

Mr. Brainard's jaw just about dropped into the water. "You did *what*?"

Old Jim shifted uneasily on his cane and swallowed. "I done it. You heard me right."

Shot a man on Main Street! That was the sort of thing Jim might have done in the old days, but good Lord, he was an old man now. And a cripple besides!

"Is he dead?"

"Couldn't say, Mr. Brainard. I hit him in the chest and he went down."

"Then he's dead. Well, hand me my bathrobe. We'd better turn you in before the sheriff comes to get you. It'll look better that way."

But a moment later, Skillety Bill Johnson, the sheriff of Hemphill County, appeared at the door. " 'Lo, Jim. Afternoon, Mr. Brainard." The men nodded. "I guess you know why I'm here, Jim."

"I reckon I do."

"You about ready to go?"

"I reckon I am."

Jim surrendered his pistol and the two men left the house. Mr. Brainard stood there for a long time, shaking his head as he thought of the tragedy. Jim Scolfield was the best cowboy he'd ever worked, and now . . . now he was a murderer and would finish out his life in a lonely prison cell. That is, if they didn't hang him first. It was very sad.

Or was it? The difference between comedy and tragedy in this story was a corpse, and as it turned out, there wasn't a corpse. True, Jim had hit the man right in the ticker, but the ticker had turned out to be his pocket watch instead of his heart. The man was bruised, stunned, and drunk, but he wasn't dead.

Can you see old Jim standing in front of Judge Baker the next day? He shifts his weight from one leg to the other and stares at the cracks in the floorboard, wishing he could turn himself into an ant and disappear into one of them. Above him on the bench towers the judge, his face a mixture of clabbered milk and Old Testament wrath. The courtroom is empty except for Mr. Brainard, who sits alone at the back, cleaning his fingernails with a pocket knife.

The judge bends forward, glaring over the tops of his spectacles. "Jim Scolfield, you old reprobate, you ought to be ashamed of yourself!"

"Yes sir."

"The very idea, getting drunk in the middle of the day and shooting a man on Main Street!"

"Yes sir, but he called me a . . ."

"Well? You can't shoot a man for speaking the truth, Jim. If I'd seen you slobbering drunk, I'm sure I'd have called you that or worse."

"Yes sir," says Jim, his head sinking deeper into his shoulders.

60

"Tell you what I'm going to do, Jim. I'm going to let you off this time, *but*," he thrusts out a long boney finger, "if you ever pull another stunt like this again, by Moses and Jesus, I'll send you so far up the river, they'll have to pack air into you with mules. Understand?"

"Yes sir."

"All right. Mr. Brainard?" He calls to the back of the room.

"Yes, Judge."

The scowl on the judge's face deepens. "Stand up, Ed, you're in a court of law."

Brainard drops his pocket knife and comes out of the chair. "Yes sir."

"Ed, against my better judgment, I'm going to give this old goat another chance, but only if you both agree to certain conditions. I'm releasing him to your custody and supervision, and these are the conditions of probation. First, he isn't to have another drop of whiskey or enter an establishment where whiskey is sold. Second, he's to meet once a week with the ladies of the Women's Christian Temperance Union, for prayer, Bible study, and discussions on the evils of drink."

Jim blinks in shock, wondering if it wouldn't be simpler if they just went ahead and hung him.

"And third, Ed, I want you to take this thing," he holds up Jim's six-shooter, "and sell it to the highest bidder and use the money to buy the best pocket watch you can find." The judge stretches across the bench and says to Jim, "In case you were worried about it, Mr. Scolfield, your friend's watch don't keep good time anymore."

Anyway, that's the way I've imagined Jim Scolfield's day in Judge Baker's court. Maybe it really happened that way and maybe it didn't. But as John Graves once said, "If it didn't happen that way, it should have."

❋   ❋   ❋

Around ten o'clock, Ed Brainard—the grandson, that is—yawned and announced that if we were going to get up at five, we'd better get some sleep. Saying good night to Ed and Lilith and the children, Bill and I made our way to the trailer and the first beds we had seen since the trip began.

Morning would come very soon, for tomorrow was roundup and branding day on the Brainard Ranch.

Working cattle in a chute is a relatively new development in the cattle business. At the Brainard roundup (left to right), Ed Brainard dehorns, Theo Mayo waits to put an age brand on the jaw, Roy B. Sessions holds the head with nose tongs, Bill McIntyre holds one vaccine gun, Bud Brainard holds another, while Ford McIntyre and Chui, a Mexican cowboy, observe the action.

IX

Roundup on the Lazy B

Dollarbill and I had gone to a big auditorium to listen to a lecture by Lawrence Ellzey, the Wolf Creek rancher. His subject for the evening was a tribe of primitive people in some faraway land. After the presentation, as my horse and I chatted with friends out in the lobby, I noticed that Dollarbill had developed a limp in his front foot. I looked it over and decided that it needed a good dose of salty meat grease, so off we went to Ed Brainard's saddlehouse. When we got there . . .

BAM! BAM!

"John? Bill? Wake up, boys, breakfast in half an hour."

For a moment I hung suspended between dream and reality, and from neither could I draw a satisfactory explanation for the voice outside the trailer. Then I heard Bill stumbling around in the other room, and my time and place began to come back to me. I lay there for a moment, waving good-bye to my dream as it climbed the hill of memory and disappeared on the other side. As my thought processes focused in on the present, I couldn't help smiling at the story my sleeping mind had concocted.

Sunrise was still a pink bud in the eastern sky and the air hung cool and soft as we picked our way across the front yard, grimacing at the feel of squashed mulberries under our feet. On the porch we paused a moment to watch Lilith through the window. Tall and attractive, with long brown hair and blue eyes, she stood over the stove in the warm yellow light of the kitchen, stirring gravy, salting calf fries that sizzled in a big iron skillet, and brushing a strand of hair back from her forehead. Then she leaned back against the counter to catch her breath and take a few swallows of coffee. We tapped lightly on the door and entered, and were met by the warm rush of kitchen smells.

Although the sun hadn't yet cleared the tops of the sand hills to the east, the murmur of young voices and the swish of bare feet could be heard in another part of the house, and now and then we caught sight of pajama-ed children, their eyes puffy with sleep, their cheeks still holding a perfect print of a pillow's topography.

After a huge breakfast of calf fries, fresh biscuits, gravy, and homemade jelly, we adjourned to the corral, and in the first glow of daylight saddled the horses and listened as Ed gave the orders for the roundup. We would be gathering two hundred cows and calves out of a five-section pasture, driving them to working pens about three miles west of John's Creek. Theo and Johnny, two Brainard cowboys from across the river, would gather the river bottom from the west. Ed and Roy B. Sessions would ride the riverbed from the east, and the rest of us, seven in all, would string out in a line a mile and a half long and push the cattle south out of the hills.

I rode right flank on the north end of the pasture, high above the meadow. It was my job to ride out the innumerable little sinks and depressions in the sand hills and push the cattle south out of my territory. Bill Ellzey, about three hundred yards below me, would then pick them up and send them on down toward the main herd which was moving slowly up the river. It was a pleasant morning. The sun had been snared in a web of high thin clouds, and a gentle breeze was blowing in from the southeast. About three miles west of John's Creek, I rode out of the hills and joined the main herd which was holding at a spring-fed pond not far from the working pens. About thirty minutes later, Theo and Johnny came in from the west with another bunch, and the herd of two hundred cows and calves was assembled.

After cutting out the bulls and dry cows, we began moving the herd toward the pens. This is the moment of truth in a cattle drive, when a rider's knowledge of cow psychology becomes crucial and the quickness and speed of his horse are tested by wily old cows who will seize on every opportunity

64

to break for open country. As eleven riders formed a cup at the rear of the herd and pushed them toward the corral gate, the whole valley filled with the noise of the drive: the general roar of bawling cattle, overlaid with the whistles and shouts of the cowboys and an occasional burst of profanity as a horse and rider engaged in a battle of wills. I still remember an epithet used by Ed Brainard that morning. He was mounted on a young green-broke horse with nothing but a bosal on his head, and at one point I heard him bellow, "Turn, you cod-headed son of a bitch!"

By this time Ben McIntyre, Ed's cousin and a partner in the ranching operation, had started a branding fire of mesquite limbs and laid out all the equipment that would be used. When the cows and calves had been cut into separate pens, the 'work began.

Back in the old days, the calves were roped and dragged to the branding fire. There were still outfits on the river that used the old method in 1972, but most had changed over to the branding table, such as the one used by the Brainards. People who use a branding table claim that it is quicker and easier on men and cattle, while those who rope and drag claim that roping is quicker and easier on men and cattle. That's the way it is in the cattle business. It's the only profession in the world where two operators can begin with opposite philosophies and come out with equally good results. Raising children may be the only other example of this phenomenon.

As I see it, the most compelling argument in favor of the chute operation is that it requires less labor. Where a crew of ten or twelve would be required to rope, throw, and work two hundred calves, a crew of five or six could work them through a branding table. And labor is a serious problem for ranchers today. Not only are wages higher than in the past, but good help is hard to find. There are probably more young men wearing cowboy boots and dipping snuff today than at any other period in American history, but most are more interested in listening to country music than in following the hard and lonely life of a cowboy.

When my great-Uncle Bert Sherman of Seminole, Texas, came to manhood in the early Twenties, he wanted to be a cowboy, and, raised on his father's ranch in Gaines County, he knew what cowboying was all about. He began his career in 1919 when he signed on with Cox and Heard west of Seminole.

Above: after the branding work is done, the cattle are driven to a spring-fed pond near John's Creek.

Below: Theo and Johnny, two Brainard cowboys, have not forgotten how the branding work was done in the old days: headin' and heelin'.

In the early Twenties he went on several long trail drives, one of which lasted a month and a half. In 1956 he hung up his spurs for the last time and retired to the old Sherman home place in Gaines County, where he now lives with his brother and sister, Roy and Olive Sherman.

In 1972 I asked Uncle Bert to write down some of his thoughts about his life as a cowboy, and he wrote the following paragraphs:

The cattle business has changed so much since I worked on ranches. For one thing the cowboys do not make the long drives we did in those days. Instead of riding ten miles to the back of the pasture to start the round-up, the boys load their horses in trailer trucks and haul them to the starting place.

I do not think cowboys today are as tough as they were years ago. They do not have the hardships to go through. Many cowboys today are on the rodeo style. If I had a ranch, would never hire a man wanting to make a rodeo his business.

Many cowboys today never stood a night guard around a bunch of cattle with the north wind blowing snow in your face, or when the rain was falling so hard you could not see a cow only when the lightning flashed. They never had to spread their beds down on the snow-covered ground, never had to eat breakfast around a camp fire at four o'clock in the morning with snow and ice everywhere.

It was a hard life, but carefree in a way. I have been bunged up, some horses throwing me off, falling on me, had some ribs broken, but not anything serious. Turned a pickup over, that hurt me more than any horse ever did.

If I was young again I would travel the same old road. There is something about the cowboy's life that gets in your blood.

Indeed, cowboying was, and still is, a hard life. Uncle Bert spent thirty-seven years in isolated cow camps in West Texas and New Mexico, living alone and working from sunup to sundown, doctoring himself when he was sick and living on a rickets and scurvy diet. And for this he was paid—what? Thirty dollars a month? Forty? I don't suppose he needed any more or had time to spend what he got. There was something else involved: maybe the adventure of living in a wild country, or the challenge of pitting one's self against animal strength and cunning day after day, or the simple pride that came in doing a job better than anyone else.

Uncle Bert's breed of cowboy has just about vanished. Today, young men who want adventure find it in the army or the Peace Corps. Those with a taste for violence (in which cowboying abounds, though it is generally directed toward animals instead of people) follow the rodeo circuit or sign on with a college football team.

A few years back, I learned on this trip, there was a kid in Canadian who wanted to be an old-time cowpuncher. He wanted it more than anything else in the world, so much that he called himself Puncher. Puncher was a town kid and had not been born into a family with land. I can imagine that around the age of fourteen or fifteen he used to sit on the curb across the highway from the Vic Mon Cafe in Canadian, watching the cowboys pull up in their four-wheel drive pickups. By the time they reached the front door of the cafe, he had analyzed and committed to memory every detail of their appearance. Did they wear Tony Lama or Nocona boots; round or sharp toes; riding heels or walking heels? He studied their hats, the width of the brim, the crease in the crown, and the amount of sweat and grime on the outside of the band. His eyes searched for clues about their use of tobacco: snuff, cigarettes, pipe, or chewing tobacco? If they chewed, he wanted to know if plug or loose leaf were in favor, and exactly how far they took their chewing: was it simply a form of entertainment, or a ritual of far deeper significance, in which case a swollen cheek and a mouth ringed with tobacco juice would become cosmetic virtues to be culti- vated. He scrutinized their swagger, their laugh, their slouch in a public place, even the way they held their forks.

There was *so* much to learn, but he knew it had to be done. Unless every ritual and gesture were studied and rehearsed, he would betray himself as a novice before the very people he wanted to impress.

He still blushed at the thought of the gigantic blunder he had pulled at last year's rodeo. After hours of waiting and watching behind the bucking chutes, he had finally managed to infiltrate a small group of bull riders, the supreme deities of the rodeo pantheon, and had even succeeded in inching his way to the very center. There, assured of the attention of heaven, he produced a pack of Kents (the first cigarettes he'd ever bought), hooked one under his lip just as he'd seen the punchers do, and offered one to the bull rider closest to him. The cowboy took one look at the brand and observed, "Hell, son, there ain't a cough in a whole trainload of them thangs," and stabbed a Lucky Strike between his lips.

By the time Puncher had gotten out of high school, he was working brandings every chance he got. Ranchers needed day labor at such times and Puncher needed the experience, and with every branding he became better and more proficient with rope and horse. But at just about the time he could have hired on with a river outfit, he received a notice from his draft board. Seems that they had a little war going over in Viet Nam and needed Puncher to help fight it.

He tried to see it in the best light. This would give him a chance to see the world and meet new people. But it was hard to rationalize, since the part of the world he wanted to see most was the Canadian River country, and the people he wanted most to meet were the cowboys who worked it.

A few days before he left for induction, he worked a branding on the north side of the river. By this time he had developed a case of nerves about going to war. "Oh boys," he wailed, "I just know I'll never make it back! I got a feeling there's a bullet over there with old Puncher's name on it." On and on he went all day long. The other cowboys just laughed and carried him high. They knew Puncher would make it back to his home range. And he did. He served his time and came back to the Canadian River country. But Puncher never made a top hand, never got the chance. After surviving the war and returning to his home range, he contracted cancer and died before he finished his twenties.

✿   ✿   ✿

By this time the work on the Brainard Ranch had shifted into high gear. The men had gotten their timing down and were running the calves through the chute at regular intervals. I found a roosting spot on top of a haystack a short distance away and settled down to watch the work.

The process of getting a calf into the branding chute began in a pen that held twenty-five or thirty head. Inside the pen were two young Mexican boys, Chui and Monsi, who kept a steady supply of calves waiting in the alley in front of the chute. I enjoyed watching these fawn-eyed cowboys, for while their approach to working cattle was clearly more exuberant than it should have been, they appeared to be having a grand old time. The calves, most of them around two hundred pounds, were just big enough to put up a respectable fight without hurting anyone. With the odds comfortably in their favor, Chui and Monsi attacked them ferociously, tossing them around the pen, cursing them in border Spanish, and stuffing them into the jaws of the branding chute. This they did with grim determination, as if ridding the world of some heinous beast, but every now and then I would catch the eye of one of them and his bronze face would blush into a boyish smile, as if I had suddenly exposed his private reverie of dragon slaying.

Once the calf had been squeezed in the chute, seven cowboys sprang into action. The calf received a cropped ear, a Lazy B on the right hip, and an age brand on the jaw; was dehorned, vaccinated twice, castrated, and daubed with fly repellent and blood stopper. Once the men had mastered their timing and the system had begun working smoothly, these eight operations were performed in about two minutes' time.

Around noon, we all drifted up to the cottonwood grove west of the corrals, watered at the spring nearby, and sat down in the shade. In a few minutes Lilith Brainard pulled up in a red four-wheel drive pickup, and shortly the pickup bed had been converted into a chuck wagon, filled with pots of red beans, potato salad, fried steak, and brownies still hot from the oven. Smiles bloomed on tired faces and a line quickly formed. The crew squatted on the ground and sat on a tree trunk and ate until there was nothing left to eat.

By five o'clock the work had been done. The calves were turned out to their mamas and the herd was driven to water. When Bill and I got back to the house, we hit the shower, put on a clean change of clothes, and drove the four-wheel drive seven miles north to supper at Ben McIntyre's place.

Ben and Nancy McIntyre lived in a handsome two-story house which sat on top of the caprock overlooking the canyons and wide valley below. At the north end of the Brainard country, Ben raised wheat, sorghum, and oats on irrigated farm land, and ran a large hog feeding operation. I often teased Ben about being a lowly hog farmer, but in fact he was every inch a gentleman: suave, handsome, articulate, and well informed on any subject, from the price of cattle to international politics— as was his wife Nancy.

Nancy was a genuine artist with food, and that night she laid out a beautiful table: an enormous roast of beef, exotic salads, vegetable dishes *au gratin*, and relish trays. Bill and I, fresh off the jerky-and-rice circuit, experienced a mild case of culture shock and protested that the food was too pretty to eat. (That was an innocent lie, because we ate plenty of it.) We filled our plates, sat down at a long Mexican table dressed with linen, silver, china, and crystal. We toasted the chef with Portuguese wine and dined by soft candlelight.

Such a meal you might expect in Paris, but when you encounter it on a horseback trip down the Canadian River, after a day of working cattle, it comes as a very pleasant surprise.

The late Woods King, the nephew of Billy Dixon and a resident of the Canadian River country for 81 years, was the unofficial historian of his piece of the world. He knew Choctaw Slim and the other moonshiners who made whiskey in the canyons north of the river, and he generously shared his stories with the author so that others might enjoy the tales and characters from this colorful period of history.

X

Canyon Rum

> "In no state in the Union was [Prohibition] welcomed so enthusiastically as in Texas. There was a sound reason for this. Under home rule the state had been partially dry; under national rule it became wholly wet."
>
> —Owen P. White, *Texas, An Informal Biography*

Early the next morning we bid farewell to the Brainards, crossed Willow Creek, and rode east into a range of high cone-shaped sand hills. After traveling for an hour or so, we came to the east fence of the Brainard land, at which point we left the sand hills and topped a rise that formed a divide between two very different kinds of country and terrain. Behind us lay gentle sloping prairies and green meadows that occasionally gave way to sand hills. Now, to the east, the big canyon country burst into our view. From that divide we could see the rims of Government, Dugout, Spring, and Sourdough Canyons; Battleship Rock and Mt. Rochester; and, some forty miles away, the brooding Blue Hills around Canadian.

As a boy growing up in Perryton, thirty miles north of the river, I was always fascinated by these canyons, which are probably the deepest and most spectacular escarpments in the northern Panhandle. I can remember, during my career as a

Second Class scout, camping and hiking in Sourdough Canyon, whose rock walls seemed a thousand feet high. Back then, the scoutmasters told us tales of Indians and panthers that had inhabited the canyons, but it wasn't until I had reached the age of twenty-eight that I heard my first tale of another species that occupied their depths: the moonshiners. Since then I have devoted a good deal of time and effort to gathering stories on this little-known but very colorful character in the history of the northern Panhandle, and I would like to suspend the journey for a moment to jot a few of them down.

In the northern Panhandle, man's relationship with liquor has always been puzzling and contradictory. That which has been drunk in private has been renounced at the polls, and as of 1977 all five counties in the northeastern Panhandle were dry. Or maybe *damp* would be more accurate, since the citizenry has demonstrated a remarkable cunning for circumventing its own legislation against the sale of alcohol. Back in the Forties, a shrewd druggist in Perryton imported a quaking old doctor and set him up in "practice." His practice consisted of writing prescriptions for whiskey which were filled out of a locked storeroom at the rear of the drug store. During the Fifties, liquor could be obtained through one of five or six bootleggers whose names were known to every school child above the age of twelve. And by the mid-Seventies, the situation had reached the level of comedy, for while Ochiltree County remained legally dry, it was also legally wet by virtue of five private clubs licensed by the state to sell liquor by the drink.

I mention all of this to point out that there have always been a few leaks in the legal dam where liquor is concerned, and also to demonstrate that times haven't changed all that much, since the same discrepancy between law and fact existed in the Twenties and Thirties, which allowed the moonshiners to function with a minimum of distractions.

When federal Prohibition struck the Panhandle in the early Twenties, it raised hackles on the necks of a people who had already prohibited themselves as far as they cared to, and who more often than not regarded Washington as the seat of Yankee imperialism. One might say that liquor didn't seem quite as odious once the federal government had decreed against it. Those who had always opposed liquor in every form now found themselves caught between hatreds, unsure of which was more deserving of their anger, John Barleycorn or Woodrow Wilson.

Those who had always enjoyed their whiskey could enjoy it more than ever now, as every swallow combined the glow of good liquor with an expression of agrarian anarchism.

So while Prohibition affected the supply of liquor, it failed to gain the moral support of the people. On the drought-stricken plains, scores of impoverished farmers, mechanics, and janitors jumped into this low-supply, high-demand market, invested a few dollars in plumbing and hardware, and set themselves up in the business of making liquor.

G. H. Holt, who ran a plumbing and tin shop in Perryton during this period, told me he probably built half the stills in the country. A customer would come into the tin shop, walk around looking at this and that, and make small talk about the weather. Finally he would get around to saying that he needed a boiler for cooking some turnips or squash, then go on to describe the dimensions of the cone-shaped device. Holt listened without comment, though he knew full well that the customer was ordering a distillery. Back in those days he got so many orders for boilers that he kept a pattern around so he could keep up with the demand. Another hot item at the Holt Tin Shop was a type of copper pan made to fit the burner of a Perfection kerosene stove, popular among the moonshiners because kerosene burned cleaner than wood and thus attracted less attention. Mr. Holt said that most of the stills he made were for small operators up in Beaver County, Oklahoma, who had turned to moonshining to keep from starving out. There were fewer orders from the Canadian River country, but the size of the boilers indicated larger operations.

Woods King once told me that during Prohibition, every canyon between John's Creek and Barton Creek contained a still, and though they were usually well concealed, their existence was not unknown to the ranchers. Mr. King explained the working agreement between the moonshiners and the landowners—and I think he was speaking from experience. "A man would come up and offer to pay you for letting him operate a distill on your land. You'd tell him, no, that could get you into trouble with the law, but if he happened to set up a distill it might be all right if he wanted to leave a quart of whiskey in your barn every month or so."

Most of these operations on the river were medium-sized, set up to satisfy a local rather than a regional thirst. Just about all of them were run by men—but then there was Sally Slocum.

I'm sure if one searched long enough, he could uncover an instance or two in which a woman engaged in the business of making canyon rum (the Weavers used to sing a song about a moonshiness named Darlin' Corey), but to my knowledge Sally Slocum was the Panhandle's only lady moonshiner. I have not used her real name, since she may have grandchildren who still reside in the Panhandle, and the grandchildren may have lawyers; but she was a real person.

Sally lived with an uncle who owned land on the flats north of the river. Against the wishes of the uncle, she married a carpenter whom we shall call Hank. Hank was not an ambitious man, and by the time Prohibition arrived he had made a botch of farming and was looking around for an easier way to make a living. The thought of peddling moonshine from his easy chair must have appealed to him, so he set up a still at the head of Couch Creek and went into business.

But Hank found working outside the law something of a strain on his nerves, and when customers came calling for his moonshine, he would tell them, "Naw, I don't have none, but maybe Sally does." This he did on the assumption that if the customer happened to be an informer from the police, and if the law happened to swoop down on the operation, they would show more kindness toward a woman than toward Hank. On this score he was probably correct, though hardly chivalrous. But then old Hank began believing his own propaganda. After a while, as the daily walk down into the canyon began to look more and more like just another form of work, he decided that since Sally was getting the credit for making the whiskey, maybe she wouldn't mind doing the work too. So he retired to the swing seat on the front porch to contemplate the mysteries of chewing tobacco, while Sally trudged off to the canyon to boil off another batch of whiskey.

Joe Day of Spearman, who used to work for the Bell Cattle Company on the river, told me he rode onto the ruins of Sally's still one day in 1931. By that time she had either worn herself out or nagged Hank into some form of employment; in any case she had retired from the business of making canyon rum.

Several years later, Hank contracted typhoid fever and died. On his death certificate there was a blank for his profession or line of work. Forty years later, it was still blank.

But Hank and Sally's business never amounted to more than nickels and dimes. The real king of the Canadian River moonshiners was a fellow called Choctaw Slim. If Slim was born with another name, something more civilized like Jim Jones or Harry Stewart, he had ceased using it by the time he came to the Panhandle. Of the five or six old-timers who described him to me, all said that he was tall, thin, and quiet. They were also unanimous on another point of description. As one man told me, "Slim was the nicest man you'd ever want to meet, but we all knew he'd kill you in a minute if you fooled around his still." From what you hear, those who fooled around his stills did it by accident and didn't tarry long.

If Slim was a bit cranky about his operation, the reason lay in his professionalism. A lot of people made whiskey during Prohibition, but few did it as well or on as large a scale as Slim. Indeed, moonshining must have been his whole life and only interest. Living alone in tents, dugouts, and shacks around the canyons; moving often to avoid detection; sleeping during the day and working nights, he seldom saw anyone and seemed content to leave it that way. He appears to have been a very rare breed of man, a genuine hermit who preferred solitude to human companionship. Of all the tales I have heard about Choctaw Slim, not one tells of a friend, a lover, or a weakness for the amusements of the flesh. As a consequence, he remains something of a ghost in the folklore of the river.

But if Slim's personality complicates the job of the folklorist, it endeared him to the businessmen who bankrolled the whiskey mills during Prohibition. To these entrepreneurs, Slim must have seemed the embodiment of the perfect moonshiner: tough, close-mouthed, solitary, and oddly dedicated to his craft. I was told that back in the Twenties a man in Ochiltree County —my informants refused to name him, as his progeny are now pillars in the community—decided to invest heavily in the whiskey business. Having established a network of suppliers and distributors, he combed three states looking for the best distiller in the land. He found his man working around Enid, Oklahoma, and his name was Choctaw Slim.

Slim became part of what must have been a very sophisticated operation. Working on a percentage basis with the boss, whom he probably never saw more than once or twice, Slim stayed down in the canyons, minding the still, and kegged the whiskey. Once every two weeks or so, a truck would inch down a treacherous road into the canyon in the dead of night and stop beside the still—or as close as a truck could get, since Slim always operated in rough, timbered terrain around seep springs at the heads of the canyons. The men in the truck worked quickly and quietly, loading up the kegs of whiskey and leaving a fortnight's supply of corn chops, sugar, and barrels. They never saw Slim, not only because his instincts sent him running into the brush at the sound of a motor in the night, but also because everyone in the operation recognized that too much curiosity and too much knowledge could get a man into trouble.

Choctaw was allowed to keep a small amount of liquor for his own purposes, which he diplomatically distributed among the local ranchers and lawmen. The rest eventually found its way to Wichita, Kansas, two hundred miles to the northeast. From the canyons, it was hauled at night and on back roads to several storage points located about fifty miles outside the city, where it was sold in small orders to a trusted group of bootleggers, who then ran it into Wichita.

It was, to say the least, a slick operation. Where the whiskey was made it was not sold, and where it was sold it was not made.

In spite of Slim's passion for anonymity, it was inevitable that occasionally his movements would be observed by the local folk. As a boy, Albert McGarraugh used to rise early of a morning to milk the cows. Many times on his way to the barn he looked off to the east and saw the glow of a lantern moving slowly up the rim of Dugout Canyon, and he knew that Slim had finished running off a batch of whiskey and was on his way to his little shack on the flats, where he would sleep until the middle of the afternoon and then maybe go out and tack up a little fence for effect. Albert's curiosity must have been whetted by this strange figure climbing out of the spooky darkness of the canyon, but not enough to overcome his fear. His father had told him that several men had walked into those canyons and never come out again.

Ben Hill, another old-timer on the river, recalled the day in the Twenties when he and his brother went up into Wright Canyon to cut cedar posts. They worked all morning cutting timber in the hot sun, and at noon they dropped their axes and walked up Hackberry Creek until they came to a deep pool of clear spring water—in which floated the rotting carcasses of three possums and a skunk. Over the pool stood a tripod with a rope and bucket attached, and a short distance away they saw three oak barrels and a boiler, beneath which the embers of a fire were still smoking. Luckily, Choctaw was nowhere in sight, though he may have had them covered from a hiding place in the cedar.

What about the dead animals in the pool? Mr. Hill theorized that they were put there by Choctaw himself, and that he used the dead animals to give his whiskey an aged flavor.

That the moonshiners along the river operated with the consent, if not the outright blessing of the landowners, is patent; that their existence in the country was known or at least rumored among the general population seems just as clear; that they were violating the law is beyond question. Then why were they not raided and run out of the country? As a matter of fact, they were raided occasionally, but the raids did not always turn out as planned.

The story of one of these raids was related to me one warm afternoon on the streets of Canadian by an old fellow named Bill Hardin. Back in 1928 Choctaw Slim was operating his still on the old Hodges place near the head of Picket Ranch Creek. One day Sheriff Johnson of Canadian and Sheriff White of Roberts County got together and decided the time had come to make a raid. Off they went in a rickety old squad car, across the river and up into the canyons. When they arrived at the scene, they found several barrels of whiskey and fresh tracks that indicated Choctaw had hooked up for tall timber. So, in the name of the law, they confiscated the liquor and headed back to Miami.

At this point in the story, Bill Hardin could hardly disguise his mirth, for more than forty years later the events of that afternoon were still vivid in his memory. The squad car containing the liquor pulled to a stop in the middle of town, and before the sun had slipped behind the bluffs along Red Deer Creek, a shocking percentage of the governments of two Panhandle counties had sampled it.

A raid in Perryton in 1931 ended with similar results. One afternoon in May, Sheriff Sid Talley received a tip that a car parked on Main Street was loaded with canyon rum. He went downtown and located a Ford coupe with out-of-county tags. Upon searching the vehicle, he discovered twenty gallons of whiskey which he confiscated and locked up in the courthouse safe, adding it to the thirty gallons he had netted in earlier raids. A week later someone broke into the courthouse, jimmied the safe, and made off with the entire fifty gallons. A news story in the *Ochiltree County Herald* reported that Sheriff Talley had no clues to the identity of the thieves. Then the editor concluded drily, "It looks like local talent may have been in on the job."

But on the whole, Choctaw Slim and his colleagues were ignored by the constabulary. The attitude of Sheriff Sid Talley of Ochiltree County was once explained to me by a man who knew him well.

"Sid was a man who was for the good of the people. He figured if the people wanted whiskey, they'd put up with the moonshiners, and if they didn't they'd run them out of the country. And another thing about Sid. He wasn't one to spend county money without good reason. He figured, why arrest the moonshiners, summon a grand jury, pay for a trial, and send them to the pen where the state would have to feed them— why do all that when the people really didn't object to the moonshiners in the first place?"

The reasoning of a very practical sheriff, who had learned to measure the righteous anger of his people against their constant grumblings over high taxes. He must have been right, because when he retired in 1944 he had held the elected office of sheriff longer than any man in Texas history.

But if the local law officers had reached a détente with the moonshiners, under which both sides understood their limits and observed certain rules of the game, the agents of the federal government honored no such agreement, and it is upon their entry on the scene that we find evidence of what comes very close to outright collusion between distillery and courthouse. Perhaps the following fictional episode, based on true stories I have heard, will illustrate the point.

Imagine, if you will, Sheriff B. J. Jones of Huntoon County, sitting in the jail one hot afternoon in July. The air inside the jail hangs heavy and still, as flies buzz in through the south window, circle the room a few times, and finding nothing of interest, exit through the open door. Jones, a peace officer in one of the world's most peaceful counties, dozes in his chair waiting for Homer Stone, the town drunk and the jail's only steady customer, to make his move at the checkerboard.

Then all at once the sheriff awakens to the sound of quick, efficient steps outside, obviously those of a stranger since no one in Huntoon is ever in that much of a hurry. He has just enough time to open and focus his eyes when in walk two men, dressed in dark suits and ties and wearing odd city-bought hats. On entering, they examine everything in the room with quick

80

sweeps of the eyes, and very poorly conceal their opinion that this is a crummy little jail in a crummy little town.

They are agents of the Treasury Department. They whip out their credentials and allow Sheriff Jones, a slow reader, just enough time to see "United Sta . . ." before they flip them shut and secret them back into vest pockets. They explain that the Department has received reports that there are several stills operating in Huntoon County, and they have orders to destroy the apparatus and arrest the offenders—who, they would remind the sheriff, are bilking the federal government of thousands of dollars in tax monies every year.

Jones reads their faces and studies their actions. He resents their condescending manner, the way they look at each other as if to share some private revelation. Obviously they believe they're dealing with a backwoods idiot, so to guard against confusing them with some glimmer of intelligent behavior, he loads his jaw with chewing tobacco, picks his ear, and gives them a lazy grin.

But at the same time his mind is racing to come up with a plan. He knows exactly where the stills are and who is running them. He also knows these are all small operators who aren't bothering anyone and who depend on their moonshine business to get along. If these federal boys go down and bust up the stills, who will feed the moonshiners' families, and who will pay their taxes?

Now, if Choctaw Slim were in the county, that might be another matter. Everybody understands that when circumstances demand that a lamb be thrown to the wolves, the honor invariably goes to Slim. For several reasons. First, he has no family to support. Second, certain anonymous individuals can always be counted upon to make bail, which saves the county the expense of boarding him in jail. And finally, he isn't a member of the county family, and while one can expend a certain amount of grief on the misfortunes of an Okie, one can certainly live with one's grief.

No question about it, a good chop and burn raid on Slim's operation could save Sheriff Jones a lot of care and worry. Unfortunately, the sacrificial lamb has recently strayed over into the pastures of Roberts County and has thus become the property of Sheriff White. That option denied him, Jones has to come up with another solution to his problem, lest these federal dudes bring pain and woe to his quiet little county.

The agents are waiting. "We thought you might like to join us, Sheriff, since this is your county and you know the back roads better than we do."

"Whaa shore," Jones replies, shifting the lump of tobacco over to the other cheek. "Ah'd be dee-latted. Them scum's been needin' a whuppin' fer a long tom. Yall come on back round dark and we'll make a raid they'll still be talkin' 'bout next Febuwary." With that, he gives them a broad brown smile.

When the agents have gone, Jones scratches his chin a moment, then walks back to Homer Stone's open cell and leans against the bars. "Homer?"

The town drunk peeks over the top of the newspaper he has not been reading for the past ten minutes, behind which his ear has been cocked to hear every word of the conversation. "Yes sir?"

"Homer, you'd like to get out of jail, wouldn't you?"

"Yes, Sheriff."

"And I'd like to get you out of jail, wouldn't I?"

"I guess so, Sheriff."

"Only the judge thought you ought to stay here for another two weeks, didn't he?"

"Yes, Sheriff."

"Well, you know, Homer, I've just been thinking. The judge is a good friend of mine and he owes me a couple of favors, and I've been sitting here all day wondering why I don't just go over to the courthouse and have a little talk about your case. I mean, you're so cooperative and everything. Know what I mean?" His brows rise significantly.

"Uh, yes, I mean, I think I know what you mean."

"I think you do too, Homer, but remember, I didn't tell you to do it. The keys are in the ignition and the gas tank's full. Tell 'em they can save the whiskey, only I want something left that'll burn. These federal boys got hot blood and they need something to catch a-fire. Now git."

Homer scrambles for the door, but as he is going out the sheriff catches him by the shirt tail. "One more thing, Homer. No drinkie de whiskey, savvy?"

Homer's face falls. "Yes sir."

That night at eight o'clock sharp, the agents return, and Sheriff Jones has the gear all ready for the expedition: three lanterns, two picks, two shovels, three axes, a sledge hammer and wedge, four crowbars, two hundred feet of heavy rope, and three Krag rifles. All of this they pile into the front seat of Jones's farm and ranch vehicle, a battered old Chevy convertible whose fenders are supported with baling wire and whose radiator bristles with impaled grasshoppers. Then, having settled the agents on lard bucket seats in the back, the sheriff gives the motor a twirl and off they go.

He takes them on the roughest and backest of the rough back roads. When they aren't fighting to balance themselves on the lard buckets and picking themselves up off the floor, the agents scowl under the flood of chatter coming from the front seat, as the sheriff expounds on bird dogs, cattle, and the beauty of the Texas Panhandle.

By the time they reach the canyons, darkness has fallen. The agents begin strapping on their gear, while the sheriff ties one end of the rope to his car. Then, loaded down like refugees, they start down the rope. Jones, ever the gentleman, allows them to go first. Then, when they have disappeared over the rim, he shucks off half his gear and follows. At the bottom, he finds them on the ground, gasping for breath and examining their blistered palms in the moonlight.

The sheriff knows the exact location of this still, but as it is only ten o'clock he figures maybe they ought to kill a little time. So, for an hour and a half, he leads them on maneuvers through the rocky, heavily wooded canyon bottom. The agents, expecting to flush out a moonshiner at any moment, follow a few steps behind, eyes probing the darkness and Krag rifles at the ready. By eleven-thirty their eyes have glassed over with fatigue, their rifle butts are dragging the ground, their clothes are soaked with sweat, and a noticeable slump has appeared in their backs.

"Cripes!" one of them rasps. "Are you sure we're in the right state?"

"Any minute now," Jones whispers, "any minute now." He heads straight for the spot near the head of the canyon.

What they find there would seem paltry in the light of day. Forewarned, the moonshiner has moved his still to another location, leaving behind a dummy operation consisting of a number two washtub, a small quantity of copper tubing, three crocks of mash, and a few footprints in the sand. But the agents are so grateful at having found *something* that they make no mention of it. While the sheriff sits on a rock and enjoys a midnight smoke, they chop, shoot, batter, and burn the operation into debris.

Around one o'clock the sheriff yawns, scuffs sand on the fire, and calls the agents to their feet for the march home. He chooses the most direct route on the return trip, but even so by the time they arrive at the rope he perceives from the wretched condition of the agents that they will never make it to the top. So he scales the wall alone and winches them out one-by-one with the car, and loads them into the back. In no time at all they have fallen dead asleep and are snoring away.

On the way back to town, the sheriff is singing the refrain of "Old Dan Tucker" when his keen eye picks up a car sitting out in the middle of a wheat field. Leaving his lights on, he walks out to investigate. The driver, he surmises, has lost control of the vehicle, left the road, crashed through a barbed wire fence, and come to rest in the field. It comes as quite a shock when, on further inspection, he recognizes the vehicle as his own squad car, and when the driver turns out to be the same Homer Stone he dispatched to the canyons earlier that day. Homer is hanging half-in and half-out the door in a position suggestive of violent death, and for a moment Jones's breath catches in his throat. But then he spies a Mason jar on the front seat and catches a whiff of the explosive vapors of canyon rum drifting up from Homer's body.

He doesn't need to be told the rest of the story. Having warned the moonshiner of the impending raid, Homer has accepted a token of the distiller's gratitude, a quart of canyon rum, and hasn't quite made it back to town. Well, at least he hasn't run into a tree or driven off a cliff. Jones drapes Homer over his shoulder and lays him alongside the sleeping forms in the back of the car and heads back to town.

Just as the first rays of light are reddening the eastern sky, Sheriff Jones pulls off his boots for the first time in twenty-four hours and lies down to catch a few hours sleep. Stretched out in bed, he reviews the day with a feeling of satisfaction. The federal boys have been properly entertained. Their reports will contain enough fluff to keep the Department content for a while. Homer Stone, his probation revoked before it has even begun, is once again lodged in the jailhouse, thus providing the sheriff with a checker partner for another two weeks. And most important, by noon a certain moonshiner will have his still going again, his livelihood spared by a benevolent county government which, come January, will have no trouble collecting his taxes.

"It all works out," thinks the sheriff, closing his eyes and releasing his grip on the world.

XI

Government Canyon

Eight hours after leaving the Brainard Ranch, we arrived at the Leroy McGarraugh place in Government Canyon, an orderly outpost of civilization thirty-five miles from the nearest town. We found the owner, Mr. McGarraugh, burning weeds out of a cattle guard with a butane torch. After swapping opinions on the weather—as I recall, the consensus was hot and dry— we stabled our animals in a very substantial set of corrals Mr. McGarraugh had built.

Constructed of heavy two-by-six planks bolted to railroad ties, these pens not only gave the appearance of being indestructible, but represented something of a marvel of engineering as well. Having built a few miles of crooked fence in my day, I could appreciate the symmetry and form of Mr. McGarraugh's creation. Given that the digging of postholes is less than an exact science, and that corral building is generally approached with functional rather than aesthetic goals in mind, it came as rather a shock to find not one gate too wide or too narrow, and not one post out of line or off center—this in a set of pens that covered half an acre.

When I mentioned this to Mr. McGarraugh, he smiled modestly and said, yeah, well he'd spent quite a lot of time on those pens—as though anyone with enough time to spare could have done as well, which I happened to know was not true. Most people I knew would simply have used more time to make

The late Leroy McGarraugh, who operated a ranch in the rugged country around Government Canyon, poses beside a machine he built in his shop. He used the machine for pulling rods and pipe out of windmills, which in this vicinity may go down as far as 400 feet to water.

more crooked fence. But if Mr. McGarraugh was not as awed by this feat of engineering as I, the reason lay in the fact that he was more accustomed to it. He was, after all, a master mechanic and builder. Given the tools and the time, he could build almost anything.

After we had stabled the animals, we climbed in Mr. McGarraugh's pickup and drove to a high mesa that stood just south of the house. We had seen it that morning from the divide on the edge of the Brainard land. From that distance it had appeared to be a cone-shaped peak, but on closer inspection we found it to be a three-tiered affair, the first step sixty or seventy feet high, the second about a hundred, and the third, which formed a point of rock about twenty-five feet in diameter, rose a hundred and fifty feet above the valley floor. Mr. McGarraugh theorized that the mountain was used as a lookout point by a culture of Pueblo Indians who lived in Government Canyon years ago, and he showed us the rock outline of a house on the second level. About twenty-four feet long and eighteen feet wide, the dwelling opened to the east and might have been used as a dormitory for sentries. From the pinnacle, they enjoyed an unobstructed view of the valley in three directions and could have observed the approach of an enemy eight or ten miles away.

In all probability, the Indians in Government Canyon belonged to the Panhandle Pueblo culture which thrived in the Canadian valley between 1000 and 1400 A.D., and which extended north to the Buried City on Wolf Creek in Ochiltree County. In contrast to the Kiowas and Comanches who came later, these sedentary people built apartment villages and diverted water courses to irrigate crops. Their houses, built of native rock and adobe, and caulked with caliche, contained no windows but were "air conditioned" by means of ventilating shafts. Although they had neither steel nor beasts of burden, they achieved a high degree of civilization and spread over a large area along the river. Why the cities were suddenly abandoned, what caused these people to vanish from the Panhandle remains a mystery, but by the time Coronado passed through the country in 1540, their cities were already in ruins.

Mr. McGarraugh had found abundant evidence of their presence on his ranch, not only several house sites, but also a quantity of fire pits, flint drills, scrapers, awls, and arrow points, mussel shells, and pieces of bone. He believed there were at least two communities in the canyon at one time.[1]

After poking around the lookout mountain for an hour, we drove north toward the head of the canyon. The south end of the canyon formed a wide sloping valley, perhaps two miles from caprock to caprock, a treeless plain bisected by the dry sandy bed of Government Creek. Up near the head, the valley floor gave way to rocks and deep washes, the walls came closer together and seemed higher, and seep springs along the creeks supported thrifty stands of cedar, cottonwood, and willow. As we drove along, Mr. McGarraugh pointed out the stumps left by government crews who entered the canyon in 1879 to cut cedar timber used in constructing a telegraph line between Ft. Elliott and Ft. Supply. We must have seen a hundred of these stumps, many of them still firm almost a century after they were cut.

Near the head of the canyon we left the pickup and walked a quarter of a mile through heavy brush and ravines until we came to a little clearing where a set of wire corrals had once stood. Though the posts had fallen down in most places, we could still walk off the perimeter of the pen and see that it had been quite large. In several spots we found hackberry trees which had been used as fence posts in the original corral, and which had completely absorbed the six wires into seventy or eighty years' growth. About twenty yards north of the pens we located a fireplace and chimney constructed of smoothed sandstone. It was here that the Askew family once lived.

Who were the Askews and why did they choose to build their house in this forbidding, almost inaccessible spot in Government Canyon? The courthouse records reveal little. In 1901 F. M. Askew paid Joe Phillips $2500 for his interest in section 154, block 13. In 1904 Askew proved three years' residency on the land. In 1906 he deeded the land to Sherman and A. M. Jines, real estate agents in Perryton. For the rest of the Askew story, we must rely on the memory of Woods King.

Mr. King could remember the old Askew place as it was around the turn of the century. The house was a wooden frame structure with a little upstairs and a stone fireplace at the north end. Around the house were a hand-dug well walled with rock, and the wire corrals.

The Kings considered Askew a tough hombre who kept bad company. Archie King, Woods's father, once told him, "There is the most dangerous kind of man you'll ever find, one who thinks up mischief but stays in the background and lets somebody else do the dirty work." That Askew had men around to do his dirty work was confirmed by the fireplace, in whose soft stones were carved three names and two sets of initials. The names were W. H. Johnson, C. Estes, and Ed Overton.

And what was the dirty work? Well, back then folks kept pretty much to themselves and didn't ask too many questions. Minding your neighbor's business wasn't always a healthy thing to do. But at the time the Askews were down in the canyon, a series of bank robberies and holdups occurred over in Oklahoma, and Judge Jack Mead of Miami once told Woods King that the Askew gang had been responsible. Another story tells of Wesley Parsell following the trail of some stolen horses twenty miles upriver and finding them two days later in a set of wire corrals in Government Canyon.

Who were W. H. Johnson, C. Estes, and Ed Overton? Woods King didn't recognize the names, and neither has anyone else I have asked. Maybe they were outlaws or moonshiners or cowboys passing through the country, and maybe we'll never know.

Another story that comes out of this part of the country occurred just a few years ago. Lyle Lloyd Brower was an itinerant ranch hand from Edgemont, South Dakota. Back in 1968 he hired on with J. M. Thrasher of Pampa as a hay hauler, just as the Thrasher outfit was moving on the Brainard ranch to cut and bale prairie hay. On Monday, after the first day's work, Brower said he was going into Pampa for groceries. He left the ranch and never came back. No one thought much about it at the time, as Brower belonged to a restless breed of men who came and went. Some were running from a dark past they never discussed, and many were in one or another stage of chronic alcoholism. One day they drifted in from nowhere, and another day, maybe tomorrow or maybe two years later, they moved on without telling anyone good-bye. Everyone assumed Brower had gotten tired of the scenery and moved on.

About two weeks later, Albert McGarraugh discovered an abandoned car sitting in his pasture. How the car got there, what the driver had been doing in that rugged country, how he had even managed to get there without four-wheel drive— these were questions he couldn't answer. He called the sheriff of Roberts County to report the vehicle and the authorities came out and towed it away. When the car was traced to Brower, the sheriff contacted Ben McIntyre on the Brainard ranch and asked if he knew anything about it. He didn't, nor did anyone else. Some of Brower's drinking chums said they had seen him in Pampa that night and that he had indulged in a few snaps of whiskey. They thought he had probably gotten lost, and when his car had stalled he had abandoned it, hiked over to Highway 70, and hitched a ride out of the country. He had pulled out, they theorized, because he didn't want to continue making payments on a car that wouldn't run.

That seemed a reasonable explanation. The car was turned over to the finance company and the case was closed.

Not long after this, Albert McGarraugh was gathering cattle in a deep canyon not far from the point at which the car had been found. As he was riding along, he noticed a number of buzzards circling in the distance. Thinking he had lost a calf, he turned his horse and started toward the spot. But then he decided against it. He was in a hurry to get the cattle moved and it was so hard to get around in that rugged country that he didn't want to waste the time. There wasn't much he could do if the calf was dead anyway, so he went on with his work.

Later that day, after he had counted his cattle and found them all there, he wondered what the buzzards had been eating. Probably just a cottontail rabbit or a dead coon.

Two years later, in the fall of 1970, a party of quail hunters was walking through the canyon and discovered a human skeleton in a sitting position, his back against a rock as though he had sat down to rest years ago and never gotten up again. Papers near the body identified him as Lyle Brower.

Apparently he had spent the evening in a bar in Pampa and had gotten a late start back out to the Brainard ranch. Somewhere along the river road he must have made a wrong turn, because he ended up in the canyon country several miles north and east of the Brainard place. Why he left the road and started driving across the pasture, no one can say, but it wasn't long until he had stuck his car in the sand. Authorities speculated that he must have seen a light in the distance and started walking toward it. He had gone about three-fourths of a mile when he stepped off a two-hundred-foot cliff and plunged to his death in the canyon below. Two years later, his remains were shipped back to South Dakota, where his parents gave him a proper burial.

❋   ❋   ❋

From the old Askew place, Mr. McGarraugh drove us from one end of his land to the other to show us five or six wire pens he had constructed over the past few years. For some time now he'd had it in his head to go into the sheep business, and he had been slowly, methodically building these coyote-proof pens to hold the sheep at night. Why sheep? He was concerned about the increase in the growth of weeds on the ranch. Cattle would not eat the weeds, and they were thriving at the expense of the native grasses. Sheep, on the other hand, would eat weeds, and after studying several large sheep operations in Mexico and the Southwest, he was convinced that running sheep on the land for a few years would improve the grass and actually make it better cattle country in the long run.

I wondered what Mr. McGarraugh's neighbors would think about his bringing sheep into the country. These days, they probably wouldn't think anything about it, but there was a time when sheep were not popular in these parts. And as a matter of fact, back in the Thirties an incident occurred only a few miles from the McGarraugh ranch that illustrated the kind of feelings sheep brought out in cattlemen who were . . . well, dyed in the wool, so to speak.

The Green family hadn't been the first to come into the river country, but they had been there long enough to put together four or five sections of grass around the canyons. This they had done by working hard, saving their pennies, and doing without many of the things they wanted. Unfortunately, they hadn't quite paid off their land by the time the drought and Depression of the Thirties hit the country. Suddenly there was no grass in the pastures, and the bottom had fallen out of the cattle market. The herd had run down and needed improving, and the note was due at the bank. Like so many other people, the Greens went under, losing everything but their two-hundred-acre homestead.

The foreclosure hit them hard. All those years of working and doing without—for what? The hardest hit was the Greens' oldest son, Norman, a man of thirty-two. Instead of going off to seek his fortune or find a wife, he had stayed on the ranch and given it the sweat of his youth. His hopes and plans for the future had all centered around ranching, on the assumption that some day the land would be his.

Norman swallowed his pride and found a job cowboying down on the river for twenty-five dollars a month, but he couldn't seem to ride far enough in a day to forget what lay behind him. Weekends would find him back at the home place, though his visits brought him little satisfaction. Like the parched grass, he seemed to be waiting for better times. He would saddle up his horse and ride down to the canyons, just to look at the country again and see how it was doing. Now he was trespassing on someone else's land, but he dared anyone to order him off. As far as he was concerned, that land still belonged to him.

One day as he rode up to the canyon rim, he looked down and saw something that made his whole body tense up. Down below, a large flock of sheep grazed along the banks of the creek. Someone had put sheep in *his canyon!* Wasn't it enough that they had stolen the land from him? Did they have to insult him further by turning it over to a sheep raiser! He spurred his horse and rode back to the house, determined that those sheep would not be there for long.

At this point it might profit us to pause and examine more closely the animosity between sheep and cattle raisers, since today the argument has lost most of its force. First, we must understand the way things were done back in those days. In isolated rural counties such as Ochiltree, Roberts, and Hemphill, law and order were preserved not so much by the sheriff as by the people themselves (Sid Talley, who was sheriff of Ochiltree County for thirty-six years, never carried a gun). There was an accepted Code of behavior, and everyone knew the Code. More often than not, the Code ran parallel to the law, although as we saw in the chapter on canyon rum, when the two were at variance, the local folk stood by their Code and left the enforcement of the law to those who had made it. The law might be broken, but the Code—no. Those who transgressed the Code in minor ways were often called before the grand jury, which in those days acted as a body of ruling elders. If the offender corrected his ways, all was forgiven. If he did not, the community moved to impose punishment, branding him an outcast.

When the offender was an adult, when he violated the Code, was properly warned and did not heed the warning, he was risking the wrath of the community. Even if the law was on his side, he could not expect the law to protect him from his peers.

And now back to the sheep. There was no law in Texas that said a man couldn't raise sheep, but it was understood that the Panhandle, and especially the river country, belonged to the cowmen. Cowmen had tamed it and fenced it and brought law and order to it, and they hadn't gone to all that trouble for a bunch of damned stinking sheep. It is ironic that a culture which worshipped the "Lamb of God" could have reserved such a thoroughgoing hatred for sheep, and one wonders how those old cowmen ever managed to get through the Twenty-third Psalm without choking.

Biblical symbolism notwithstanding, sheep were roundly despised. For one thing, it was accepted as fact in those days that sheep would graze the grass right down to the roots and ruin the country for three or four years. Sheep also demanded a kind of care that no self-respecting cowman could regard as anything but contemptible. They took a man off his horse and set his feet in the dust, and in a country where men were often measured by their horsemanship, this was not popular. And finally, the animal itself seemed deserving of contempt. Sheep were short-legged, soft-nosed, and roly-poly; they stank, made insipid little noises, and were given to heart failure at the sight of a prowling coyote.

It should come as no surprise, then, that sheep raising was forbidden under the Code.

And so we have Norman Green riding back to the house, leaving his horse standing in the corral, jumping into the nearest vehicle, and roaring down the road to Perryton. When he got there, he made a few inquiries and learned that the bank had leased the canyon pasture to a man we shall call Harley Stafford. Norman found Stafford and told him to get his sheep out of the canyon. No doubt Stafford laughed in his face and told him to mind his own business. Perhaps there were threats and counterthreats, and the two parted in anger.

Norman Green had driven to Perryton in the heat of anger, but as he drove home he noticed the anger had cooled and he felt strangely at ease, almost as though the matter had already been settled. And in a way it had. Stafford had broken the Code. He had been warned. Now all that remained was to see that justice was done.

Back at the house, Norman went to the hall closet and brought out his Winchester. Ignoring the questioning looks of his parents, he strode out the door, got on his horse, and rode down to the canyon. Three hundred yards below, he could see the herder sitting on a rock and chewing a stem of grass.

93

Norman cocked a bullet into the chamber, drew a bead, and pulled off five quick shots. Five plumes of dust erupted in a circle at the herder's feet. The sheep bolted and ran. Stunned, the man looked down at his feet and up to the canyon rim, then in a flash he was gone, ducking behind thickets and rocks as he made a dash up the west fork of the canyon.

Well, thought Norman, that was the end of that.

But Harley Stafford was a stubborn man and not the sort to back off from a fight, especially when he figured he had a perfect legal right to run sheep anywhere he pleased. So he found another sheepherder and put him down in the canyon. And the next weekend Norman Green returned with his rifle and sent the man fleeing into the brush. This continued for several weeks, until Stafford had run through the local supply of sheepherders and could not find anyone willing to venture into the canyon.

No doubt while all this was going on, friends of Stafford told him to give it up, pointing out what was obvious to everyone else in the county, that he had chosen to make a stand on the wrong issue and that public opinion was against him. To which he probably replied, "Damn public opinion! Running sheep is as legal as going to church, and nobody's going to stop me." And so the very next day he drove to Amarillo and found a tough Mexican fellow who was looking for work. Could he be scared off? The man smiled and shook his head. He wasn't scared of nuthin, and nobody was going to run *him* off. Stafford hired him on the spot and left him in the canyon that night, confident that Norman Green had finally met his match.

The next weekend Green rode up to the canyon rim, saw the new herder, pulled out his rifle, and shot a circle around his feet. Sitting with his arms folded, the Mexican cast a lazy glance at the craters in the ground, looked up at the rifleman, and gave him a mocking grin. So Norman reloaded and fired off another volley. The Mexican was still grinning up at him. Years later, Norman Green told a close friend what happened next. "I shot and shot and he never even moved, so finally I just cut down on him." He shot him dead.

About a week later, Stafford went down to the canyon to see how his new man had fared. He found the decomposing body just where it had fallen and the sheep scattered all over the river country. This was enough to convince him that the sheep business was going to be too expensive for him, so he rounded up what was left of his flock and pulled out of the canyon. Two hundred sheep were never found, victims of coyotes—and unfriendly ranchers.

An old man in Perryton told me this story and claimed he heard it straight from the mouth of the man I have called Norman Green. He didn't use real names because the murder was never solved and the case never went to trial. Why? Maybe because the sheepherder was a Mexican. Maybe because he came from the outside. Maybe because he didn't have family around to push for a more vigorous investigation. My informant gave this further explanation:

"This was the most peaceful county you can imagine. We never had any trouble around here, and had damned few trials. People respected the Code and lived by it. But when somebody broke the Code and tried to run over people, you could expect a killing. That's what happened to the Mexican. The man who killed him didn't have anything against him personally; he was just working for the wrong side and had to be eliminated. Nothing was ever done about it because people felt like everybody had got what they deserved. The killing was justified."

❁   ❁   ❁

By nine-thirty that evening we had seen the last of Mr. McGarraugh's sheep pens, and he turned the pickup toward home. By this time the lunch of jerky and raisins we had taken at noon that day had left Bill and me, and we had grown weak with hunger. Bill dozed in the middle, while I slumped against the door and tried to hold up our end of the conversation, grunting monosyllables except when pressed. We arrived at the house none too soon, staggered into the dining room, and found the table loaded down with plates of hot food, upon which we fell like two starved coyotes in the dead of winter. Mrs. McGarraugh's good cooking saved us, and at ten-thirty we said good night and made our way down the hill to the little bunkhouse, where we spread out our bedrolls on the springs of two roll-away cots. We had spent an interesting afternoon in Government Canyon, and tomorrow we faced a hard twenty-mile ride to Jim Streeter's place on Point Creek. With a gentle rain sizzling on the roof, we turned out the light and crawled into the covers.

Characters in the drama that unfolded on June 24: Suds, Erickson, Dollarbill, and Dobbin, the Bolshevik Mule. They are observed by a bullfrog,
who is a big frog in a little pond.

XII

Dobbin Is a Communist

We rose at six the next morning and went right to work putting our gear in order for the trip. Around seven Mrs. McGarraugh called us to breakfast and we dropped our work and went to the house.

We had hoped to get an early start on the day, but at the breakfast table good coffee and good companionship conspired to hold us longer than we had planned. After the meal, the conversation turned to horses and Mr. McGarraugh told us about a horse he had ridden in his youth. "He bucked for a whole mile and I stayed with him, but I'm not sure it was worth it. When I got down, I was bleeding from the nose and ears." He took a swig of coffee. "Boys, you can never trust a horse, no matter how gentle he seems to be."

I nodded, thinking of how gentle Dollarbill seemed to be.

By eight-thirty we had loaded the animals and reported to the front of the house for some last minute picture taking. Mrs. McGarraugh emerged from the house with a little Kodak camera and told us to pose beside the animals. Mr. McGarraugh stood on the sidelines, tapping his toe and gazing mournfully off to the east, as if calculating the height of the sun against the work he had planned for the day. Then the order came down for *him* to get into the picture. He grumbled and muttered in protest and took up a rigid position beside Dollarbill, where he continued to scowl out at the prairie.

"Look this way," said Mrs. McGarraugh, squinting into the viewfinder. We obeyed, but Mr. McGarraugh just pulled his hat down further over his eyes. "Leroy! Look this way." Finally he swung his eyes around and glared at the camera. "Smile." Bill and I were laughing by this time, but Mr. McGarraugh never did crack a smile.

We said good-bye to the McGarraughs and rode south down the county road. We looked into the coming day with nothing but dread. Not only were we getting a late start, but half a mile down the road Bill noticed a slight limp in the mule's front legs, a sure indication that he had developed sore feet the day before. This observation plunged us both into a gloomy silence, and for a while we even considered turning back. But we decided to go on, and resigned ourselves to a creeping twenty-mile march across the burning prairie in the heat of the day.

When we left the McGarraugh land, we entered the Lipps Ranch, one of the largest ranches in the northern Panhandle, and one which had known only two owners since the 1880s: the lady from down-state who owned it then, and an old codger named Bill Whitsell who put the ranch together. A bachelor who lived alone in a house called Red Camp, Whitsell managed to assemble more land than any other man in the region, and in the process built up a reputation for being as tight as the bark on a tree. He worked hard, lived on bacon and beans, hired outside help only when it was absolutely necessary, and showed no mercy in his land deals.

Whitsell was an expert on how little protein supplement a cow needed to survive the Panhandle winter. They say that after a big blizzard he would throw a sack of cottonseed cake over the saddlehorn and ride out to check his cows. Those he found standing were presumed to be healthy and fit, and he wasted no time on them. When he came to a cow that was lying down, he would gallop straight toward her, shouting and waving his arms. If she managed to stagger to her feet, he figured she could stagger some more and find enough forage to survive. If she was too weak to stand, he threw her a handful of cake and went on.

For years Whitsell lived alone at Red Camp, eating his beans and socking away every dime he didn't put into land. Then one fall he shipped a load of cattle to Kansas City. By this time he was a shriveled old man with gray hair and sagging skin, who probably resembled his own cows after a hard winter. He had more land than he could take care of and more money than he knew how to spend, and though the decision came rather late in his life, old man Whitsell vowed he would find some excitement in Kansas City. He went to a dance hall. We don't know what happened there, whether he was blinded by bright lights and liquor, or whether his eyes were opened to a side of life he had never known before. The next time we see him is at the depot in Canadian, as he helps a young lady with fiery red hair down from the train. Dressed in a green velvet gown with hat and parasol to match, she beams a simple little smile at the local folk, who are suddenly stumbling over baggage, running into walls, and staring in amazement at this painted woman.

The old rancher, dandied up in spats, bowler hat, and the first suit anyone has ever known him to wear, takes the lady's arm in his and turns a smiling face toward the crowd. "Folks, it gives me great pleasure to present to you . . . the new Mrs. Whitsell!"

Jaws come unhinged, palms smack foreheads, and maybe at the back of the crowd someone falls in a dead faint.

"And now, Joe," Whitsell says to the porter, "if you'll take care of our baggage . . ." He points to ten steamer trunks along the siding.

"All of them, sir?" the porter gulps.

"That's right," Whitsell chuckles. "The rest of Kansas City wasn't for sale."

In Canadian in 1972 there were several sweet little ladies who remembered the day old Whitsell brought his bride to town. Although they spoke kindly of her, it was clear from their careful choice of words that her appearance in Canadian created something of a scandal. Some spoke of Mrs. Whitsell as a very nice woman. Others said the same, but added, "in spite of her problem." She drank a lot. Still others pointed to her interest in culture and music; she played the trombone and was considered quite good.

And then there was the story about the robbery. I heard two versions of it. One day Mr. and Mrs. Whitsell were motoring down the river road between Canadian and the ranch. Near Mt. Rochester, where the road cut through a gap, they were stopped by two bandits, who, at gunpoint, demanded money and all of Mrs. Whitsell's jewels. Here, each of my informants drew his own conclusion to the story. The first thought it shameful that the bandits were never caught. The second believed that Mrs. Whitsell was lucky she didn't go to prison over it, since she had engineered the whole scheme to collect a potful of insurance money on a few strings of glass beads.

But everyone agreed on one point: Mrs. Whitsell taught her old man how to spend his money. Under her tutelage, he moved out of his shack on Dugout Creek, purchased the biggest home in Canadian, and furnished it out of the best shops of Europe. They sailed around the world and Mrs. Whitsell wore the most expensive clothes everywhere she went. To the local folk, it must have appeared that the old man had fallen into the clutches of a scheming, ambitious big-city woman. He may have, but from what I have heard, no one ever enjoyed the schemes and ambitions of a big-city woman any more than Bill Whitsell did. He seemed right proud of his dance hall queen.

✿　✿　✿

After following the county road four miles south, Bill and I came to the spot at which it intersects the river road, where we met Woods King on his way out to the ranch with a load of feed in the back of his pickup. We stopped and chatted a while. Mr. King took a long look at Suds and said he was a fine-looking horse. I waited for him to say the same about Dollarbill, my donkey-faced friend, but he didn't. He turned to the mule and said he thought Dobbin had sore feet. When he had gone on down the road, Bill and I wiped the sweat off our brows, swung up into the saddle, and prepared for what we presumed would be a hot uneventful ride.

We had gone about a quarter mile east of the road intersection. The sun hung directly overhead like a ball of white fire, roasting every fine and beautiful thought out of my head and leaving me with nothing to contemplate but plague, famine, and the other miseries of existence. My arm ached from holding the halter rope, at the end of which the mule chugged along at his damnable pace.

"Bill," I said, "you ready to mule it for a while?"

Without the slightest glimmer of enthusiasm, my partner nodded, took the rope, and began the task of trying to winch another few feet per hour of speed out of the long-eared corpse we called Dobbin. And I drifted out on a hot sea, bobbing up and down with the waves in very much the same rhythm one might find on a slow walking horse on a hot summer day on a sandy road somewhere in Texas.

I don't know what happened to Dollarbill. Maybe he saw a lizard. Maybe he fell asleep and awoke with a start. But all at once I felt myself flying through the air and opened my eyes just in time to see the earth rushing toward me. An instant later I crashed on hands and knees on what must have been the hardest graded road in Roberts County. Dollarbill, my kind and gentle companion, had just humped up and bedded me down. ("Boys, you can never trust a horse, no matter how gentle he seems to be.") Dollarbill bolted to the left and headed west in a run.

As I mingled with the dust from which we all have sprung, Dobbin, our Bolshevik mule, sensed the moment had arrived for agitation. Charging forward, he jobbed Suds in the behind with his head and very adroitly snarled the halter rope around his hind legs, a strategy we had seen on John's Creek three days before. You can fault Dobbin for lack of imagination but not on results. Suds snorted, broke in half, and bucked to the left. Bill didn't try to hold onto the mule this time, but that didn't save him. The first jump threw him off balance, and although he grabbed for everything in sight—mostly air and sunshine— on the third jump he slipped over the right side and joined me at the very lowest and humblest level a horseman can know. Two jumps later, we were joined by his four hundred dollar Nikon.

When the dust had cleared, I glanced to my right and saw the holes in the bottoms of Bill's boots staring back at me. "Can't you stay on that horse?" I asked.

"Who fell off first?" he shot back.

"That's beside the point. You're supposed to be an explorer or something, but every time I look around you're falling off your horse."

I don't recall what he said to that, and probably couldn't repeat it if I did.

The animals had stopped about two hundred yards to the west and were regrouping to plot their next move. Bill and I dusted ourselves off and talked it over. We knew if the animals ran, we were in for a very long day. After giving them a few minutes to settle down, Bill started toward them. As expected, the mule began slinking away, but luckily the horses didn't follow his example. Heads up and ears cocked, they watched

Bill approaching. A moment later he had a bridle in each hand and was leading them back to the scene of the wreck.

This put the mule in an awkward position, for while he had not the slightest affection for Bill and me, he prized the company of the horses. Once they had surrendered and were being led back, he glared after them, then reluctantly followed a safe distance behind. Bill gave me the horses and went back to capture the mule. Dobbin took evasive action, keeping his rump toward Bill, running a few steps and stopping, and scouting the rear with a wary eye. Finally Bill managed to catch him, but by this time my partner's sense of humor had soured in the heat, and when, as they came back down the road, Dobbin suddenly planted his feet and refused to walk another step, Bill rebuked him in a voice they could have heard all the way to Sam's Corner, and gave the halter rope a jerk. You can do that with most horses and get by with it, but Dobbin refused to take punishment of any kind, and now he threw a fit. Bill held on as long as he could, but having no desire to take another Panhandle sleigh ride through the sagebrush, he dropped the rope and let him go.

Free again, the Communist mule went to work on the pack saddle. He coiled his hind legs under him and kicked for the moon. We watched as the pack saddle inched down his right side. We knew if the load ever got down between his legs, we wouldn't have enough saddle and gear left to fill our pockets. Farther and farther down the load slipped, until it hung almost under his belly. One more jump and it would be.

But then he stopped bucking, swished his tail a couple of times, and started cropping grass, with the load protruding from his side like an enormous tumor. Who can explain the behavior of animals? Fifteen minutes earlier, Dollarbill had started bucking for no apparent reason, and now Dobbin had ended it, just as suddenly and mysteriously. It didn't make sense then, it doesn't make sense now, blessed be the name of the Lord.

XIII

Dave Wilson

The hours crawled by. Around noon we passed the old Red Camp place, which is no longer red, crossed Highway 70 under the Dugout Creek bridge, and pushed on into the most uninspiring country we had seen. Maybe the heat had something to do with it—it was miserably hot and still—but I shall always harbor unpleasant memories of that stretch of country between the highway and Point Creek. It was flat, barren country with bone dry creeks and sandy roads that reflected the angry rays of the sun back into our faces.

On and on we rode, not daring to look back lest we be plunged into despair at how far we hadn't come. Sweat rolled down our cheeks, deer flies droned overhead, and in front of us lay an endless prairie blazing white in the afternoon sun. For hours we hardly spoke a word. Even if we'd had the energy to talk, which we didn't, our conversation would have returned to the heat, the sand, the cursed flies, the stillness and desolation that lay all around us—subjects which didn't need discussing. And so we bobbed along, trying to occupy ourselves with other thoughts.

Slumping in the saddle, I gazed off to the north where the prairie suddenly gave way to the caprock that rose two hundred feet into the air, forming sheer rock walls and deep canyons. That was Dave Wilson's country. With nothing better to do, I tried to remember all the tales I had heard about Dave Wilson.

The rugged canyon country north of the river, near the ranch where old
Dave Wilson established himself as one of the best ropers the river ever
produced.

Down on the river, when the conversation turns to roping, it either begins or ends with Dave Wilson, one of the best ropers the country ever produced. In his youth, Dave used to drive cattle from New Mexico to the Wilson ranch north of the river, a distance of several hundred miles. To pass the long hours in the saddle, he would practice heeling, throwing one loop after another, hour after hour, day after day, until he could hit just about anything he threw at. In his hands a rope became more than a piece of line; it was a specialized tool with which he could perform a number of jobs. For some jobs he threw for the head, for others the horns, heels, or forefoot. He always rode a good roping horse, and the first thing he did when he mounted up was to make a big loop in his rope and lay it over the saddlehorn.

Back in the Twenties, when times were hard and money was scarce, Dave would enter rodeos to pick up a little extra cash. Leaving home with three horses, he would ride all the way to Campo, Colorado, to rope in a rodeo. He would take his bedding, a skillet, some bacon and flour, and camp out along the way. At night he would build a fire, fry the bacon and add flour, salt, and baking powder to the grease, making a kind of hoe cake. He would return home five or six days later with as much as a hundred dollars, having won first money in calf and goat roping.

The first year Mr. Studer of Canadian brought in Brahman bulls for his Anvil Park Rodeo, one of the bulls jumped the corral fence and headed west. Four or five cowboys gave chase and tried to get a rope on him, but they couldn't do it. My own guess would be that they didn't want to very badly, a sentiment I understand completely. The bull continued west at a run, and a few days later Mr. Studer received word that he had been spotted in Ochiltree County, about thirty miles northwest of Anvil Park. Studer's next move was to pay a visit to Dave Wilson to see if he would rope the bull. Dave said he wasn't afraid of the bull and that he would see what he could do. So he and Mr. Studer loaded the best roping horse on the place and drove out to find the bull.

Perhaps movies and television westerns have dulled our capacity to appreciate feats of cowboy daring, so I would like to emphasize just how dangerous an undertaking this was. If Dave Wilson wasn't afraid of roping the bull, he probably should have been. In the first place, suppose he missed his first loop and the bull turned on him? Very simple, you say, he would just give his horse the spurs and away they would go. Maybe, but maybe not. I would imagine that Dave's horse was big and stout. A horse big enough to hold a full grown Brahman bull would *have* to be, and one that weighed twelve or thirteen hundred pounds might not be very fast. A charging bull with just a second's head start could easily catch him. And if that happened, the bull could knock the horse off his feet, and possibly gore him with a horn.

And there's another point to consider. Dave's strategy was to catch the bull by the forefoot instead of the head, for obvious reasons: the bull probably outweighed the horse by at least five hundred pounds, and maybe even as much as seven or eight hundred. Instead of taking on the bull in a contest of strength against strength, Dave intended to catch the front leg and use leverage and cunning to defeat him. But catching that front hock was a nifty trick. A sudden gust of wind, a small miscalculation, or an unexpected movement in the bull could put Dave's big loop around the neck instead of the front hock. And if the bull was tied hard and fast to the horn—and I think most ropers of his generation preferred tying hard and fast over dallying—then Dave would have a horse at one end of the rope and a much heavier bull at the other, strength against strength with all the advantages on the bull's side. If the bull ever hit the end of the rope, he could jerk the horse off his feet, and any cowboy who has ever been in this position will shudder at the thought of what could happen then. It is a cowboy's nightmare: an angry bull, a floundering horse, a man on the ground, and thirty feet of hissing rope among them.

So when Dave Wilson agreed to rope the bull for Mr. Studer, he took on a dangerous job.

When they spotted the bull, Dave put his usual big loop in the rope and rode out across the pasture. The bull ran, and Dave fell in behind him, waiting for the right moment and position as the rope whistled over his head. In an instant he made a dozen calculations about speed and distance and the location of the bull's front leg, and then he threw. It was a perfect shot. When he saw the loop pull tight on the hock, he flipped the rope, turned his horse to the left, and waited for the slack to run out. When the bull hit the end of the rope, his front legs were jerked out from under him and he fell with a thud to the ground. Angry now, he leaped to his feet and prepared to charge, but before he had a chance Dave flipped the rope again, put his horse toward the proper angle, and threw him again. Snorting and bellowing with rage, the bull tried again and again to charge the horse, but each time, with a flick of his wrist and a few steps to the side, Dave sent him sprawling to the ground.

Finally the bull hit the ground and didn't get up. Slobbering at the mouth and heaving for breath, he lay there, conquered by a man one-tenth his size. Then Studer's cowboys moved in, roped his hind legs, stretched him out, and wrapped him up in good stout rope. (And while this was going on, I can see Dave Wilson lounging in the saddle, one leg hiked over the horn, and maybe scratching a splash of manure off his boots with a pocket knife.) When the bull had been tied down, Studer's men dug a pit beside him and backed a truck into it. Threading ropes through heavy steel rings that had been welded at the front of the truck bed, they began inching the bull into the back. Then Mr. Studer walked over to Dave and handed him a check for forty dollars—more than a month's cowboy wages for an hour's work.

Old Dave wasn't any more afraid of rattlesnakes than he was of the bull. When he came upon a rattler he would wave his hand over the buzzing coil, then slowly reach down and pick him up with his bare hands. He used to tell his boys, Elrick and David, Jr., that the only time a man ought to be afraid of a rattlesnake was during mad dog days in the fall, when the snakes are blind.

I heard another good yarn on Dave Wilson. It seems that he was one of the first men in the county to own a pickup truck, a rather crude vehicle by modern standards, since it had just a flat bed without sideboards or stock racks. Most people would have used it for hauling cake and hay, but Dave wanted it for something else. He wanted to haul his horse around in it. Or rather, *on* it. When he needed to check some cattle in a pasture a few miles away, he would jump his horse up on the flat bed and away they would go.

Now, Dave Wilson might have been one of the best ropers in the country, but no one has ever bragged on his driving. Of course a cowman had other things to look at besides the road when he was driving. He had to study the grass and the cattle and the clouds, and somehow old Dave never managed to find time to watch where he was going. Curves sneaked up on him, holes appeared out of nowhere, and fences just seemed to jump into his path.

It wasn't at all uncommon for Dave to look up and see some kind of catastrophe awaiting him ahead. As long as he avoided trees and canyons, this was fine—for the driver. But for the poor horse, every ride on the pickup bed must have been a story of horror and chilling suspense. With his legs benched at the knees and spraddled to all four points of the compass, his head hung low, his tail tucked between his legs, he patiently absorbed the jolts and leaned into the corners as the truck went bouncing across the pasture. But Dave's driving defied reason or logic. Just as the horse had learned to lean left when the road curved left, Dave would see a cow standing out in the pasture and whip the truck to the right. Just when you thought he would accelerate, he would stomp on the brakes. When you knew he would swerve left to miss a hole up ahead, he would plow right into it.

The horse tried, Lord knows he did, but now and then it was inevitable that he went one direction and Dave and the truck went the other. And of course Dave, who knew he wasn't the smoothest driver in the world, would be very understanding about it, right? Naw. He'd come boiling out of the cab, kick the horse in the rump, and bellow, "Damn you, can't you stand up!" And the poor horse, twice shamed, would struggle back up on the platform and prepare himself for another nightmare ride.

❂   ❂   ❂

Well, I had recalled all the Dave Wilson stories I had ever heard. It was still miserably hot and the locusts were droning all around us. Up ahead, Bill looked as though he had been shot through the heart and just hadn't fallen out of the saddle yet. Dobbin seemed to be walking slower by the hour. I tried to shut out the harsh world around me and think of ice tea and cold watermelon. It didn't work.

XIV

The Angel of Picket Creek

Around three o'clock in the afternoon we opened a pasture gate and rode onto the Killebrew ranch. We had spent eight straight hours in the hot sun. Our canteens were dry. We hadn't eaten, and our horses hadn't drunk since eight o'clock that morning. Ours was a sad little caravan heading down the road.

But we didn't have far to go this time, for up ahead about half a mile was the headquarters of the Killebrew ranch where we could stop for water and a little rest. As we made our way toward the well house, the Killebrews' hired man—I believe his name was Robert Smith—came out to greet us, turned on the pressure pump, and told us to drink all we wanted. When we had taken on a full load of water, we went down to the corral to stable the animals.

By this time another man, Robert Smith's brother, had come out to see us. As I buckled my spurs together and hung them over the saddlehorn, he gave them an admiring look and asked if I wanted to sell them. I told him that my Grandfather Curry had made them on a coal forge many years ago, using good heavy steel and decorating them with Mexican centavo pieces. My grandmother had given them to me so that I could use them on the Canadian River trip. I was very proud of them, and no, I wouldn't sell them for any amount of money.

Down at the corral, we unloaded Dobbin and turned him and the horses into a water pen. I thought at the time about

109

Jim Streeter, the "Angel of Picket Creek."

unsaddling Dollarbill, but I didn't because I was too tired and hungry. Later, I would regret that decision.

We hiked back up to the house, settled down in the grass under the shade of a tree, and lunched on jerky, raisins, and water, which we shared with a multitude of frenzied little ants. We were sitting in the front yard of Carrie Palestine Killebrew's house. I never had the pleasure of meeting Mrs. Killebrew— death took her about six months before I began doing research for the river project. Everyone I met in the fall of 1971 told me, "It's too bad you didn't have a chance to talk to Mrs. Killebrew. She could have told you a lot about this country. She'd been living on the river since 1890." She must have been a strong woman, because at the age of eighty-one she was still living alone on the ranch, doing her own housecleaning and taking care of herself just as she always had.

Maybe it was inevitable that something would happen to her. It came in February of 1971, during the worst blizzard of the decade. For two days and nights it snowed. A strong north wind piled two feet of snow into drifts that buried cars, houses, fences, and roads, and left the northern Panhandle completely paralyzed. Mrs. Killebrew was alone on the ranch, and during the blizzard she fell and broke her hip. She managed to crawl to the telephone and call her son Walter in Canadian for help. But Canadian was buried. Traffic had come to a complete standstill. The sheriff's office at Miami called Jim Streeter, the nearest neighbor, on the two-way radio to see if he could reach the Killebrew place, but the storm was raging down on the river and there was nothing he could do.

Finally, when the storm broke two days later, a National Guard helicopter from Amarillo landed at the ranch and Mrs. Killebrew was flown to Highland General Hospital in Pampa. But she never recovered from the accident, and in late March she died.

We lounged in the shade for thirty minutes or more, slowly gaining back some of the energy we had lost during the ride from Government Canyon. Then we tied up the jerky and raisin bags, filled our canteens, and started down to the corral. When we passed out the yard gate, we noticed a red Ford pickup parked out in the drive and heard the Smith brothers talking to the driver about cattle. I didn't recognize the man in the pickup. In fact, I couldn't see anything of him but a wide brimmed straw hat with a long nose beneath it. But as we

111

drew closer, he cocked his head back and I saw that it was Jim Streeter. I didn't recognize him immediately because I had seen him only once before. While making preparations for the trip, I had gone down on the river to ask his permission to cross the Tandy ranch and to see if it would be all right for us to camp a night or two around his place. I had gone down to see him not once but eight times, only to learn that he was somewhere else every time. Finally, about a week before we left on the trip, I located him in a conference with a windmill crew up on the flats.

But he knew who we were and asked if it was warm enough for us. We said it was, and then we did some moaning about the mule. "How far is it to your place?" I asked, thinking in terms of three, maybe four miles.

"Oh, about seven miles."

Bill and I gasped. It seemed we had been traveling forever, only to learn that we still had five and a half hours left in the saddle.

"You boys will eat supper with me, won't you?" Mr. Streeter asked. We allowed as how we would be delighted, providing we got there before morning. "Good. Now, my wife's gone for the weekend and I'll be doing the cooking, so you'll have to take your chances."

We trudged down to the corral to get rigged up for the ride. When we had loaded Dobbin and left him tied outside the gate, I caught Dollarbill and discovered that he had rolled in the dirt while we were gone—with the saddle on. The dirt I could live with, but it ate my liver that he had rolled over the ancestral spurs of which I was so proud, and had mashed the left one so badly that it would no longer fit on a boot. I could have murdered him in cold blood.

Finally we got under way. In the first quarter mile we learned to our grief that we had wasted our consideration on the mule. Having rested and watered for thirty minutes, he now set a pace that would have shamed a snail. Before long, Jim Streeter passed us on his way home, and as he drove by I noticed that he was scrutinizing Dobbin pretty carefully. We gave a half-hearted wave and sank back into our misery.

Around five-thirty we came to the dry sandy bed of Picket Ranch Creek, about two and a half miles east of the Killebrew headquarters. Just as we climbed up on the other side, we looked down the road and saw Jim Streeter's pickup coming toward us.

He was pulling a stock trailer. We figured he was going down to one of the river pastures to bring in a sick calf. He pulled up beside us and stopped.

"How you doing?" he asked.

"Swell."

He nodded. "I thought maybe you boys would like to unload that mule and put the gear in the pickup. He might move a little faster without a load. I don't think he has any race horse in him, does he?" That drew a laugh. "Well, you boys do what you want, but I'll be glad to take your gear back in the pickup."

"What do you think, Bill?" I asked.

"I don't know. What do *you* think?"

What we both thought was that we had set out to make this trip in the old way. We could have made it by Jeep or motorcycle, but we had chosen to travel the way people traveled in the 1880s and 1890s, and to do it with a minimum of cheating. But now we were confronted with the temptation of convenience, and the day had left us vulnerable to philosophical impurities. So we sparred around for several minutes, neither sure of what the other thought, and both of us secretly wishing the other would come out and say, "Yes, yes, take it!"

Finally, we more or less backed into the decision to send the gear ahead in the pickup.

Pulling on his ear and gazing up at the sky, Mr. Streeter said, "Now I don't want to butt into you boys' business, but you're welcome to send the *mule* back too. Looks to me like he's got sore feet."

This sent us into another flurry of soul searching. Sending the gear back was a small concession, but one which would still allow us a triumphant procession into Mr. Streeter's corrals at the end of the day. Sending the mule back would be a clear and undeniable breach of philosophy, an admission that we weren't as rugged as those old-timers. We squirmed and writhed with this painful decision.

But . . . the mule's feet were sore, and without him to slow us down we could make better time on the horses. And we did have an invitation to supper.

We loaded Dobbin into the trailer.

Mr. Streeter closed the gate, hooked his thumbs in his belt, and kicked up a few rocks with his boot. "Course, as far as that goes, there's plenty of room in the trailer for your horses. They look pretty tired. But like I say, that's strictly your business."

113

I looked at Bill and Bill looked at me. I expected to see him recoil in horror at this suggestion, but maybe he had reached about the same point I had reached. I was just flat too tired to recoil in horror. He grinned and I grinned. Well hell's bells, as long as we'd compromised ourselves on two points, we might as well be consistent and go down a third time.

We loaded the horses and headed for the house.

I had never thought that compromise and defeat could be so sweet. As we rode toward the ranch, I hung my head out the window and let the cool breeze dry the sweat on my face and head, and all at once the country didn't seem nearly as brown and harsh as it had appeared on horseback.

And then there was Jim Streeter to make the day even better. I had been around him not more than twenty minutes in my whole life, yet already I had developed an enormous liking for him. I realized now why he had come back. What he had seen at the Killebrew place must have convinced him that we had had enough for one day, that both we and the animals had just about exhausted ourselves. But the fact that he had somehow understood our pride and stubbornness touched me. And we *were* proud and stubborn. If necessary, Bill Ellzey and I would have crawled on our bellies that last seven miles. We would have endured sunstroke and snakebite and the seven plagues of Moses, but we would have arrived at our destination. You say that the point wasn't worth making? We thought it was, and I believe Jim Streeter thought it was too, only wise man that he was, he realized that the point had already been made and it was time to call it a day.

I attended Sunday School and church regularly in my youth and gained quite a bit of exposure to the Bible, but no one ever told me that an angel could wear a straw hat and drive a red Ford pickup.

114

XV

The Tandy Ranch

When we got to the ranch house, we unburdened the animals and Mr. Streeter put them into stalls and fed them some sweet feed. Dollarbill didn't deserve such good treatment after bucking me off and rolling on my spurs. Outside the lot, I walked over to Mr. Streeter, who was unhitching the trailer, and decided to get his opinion on what I should do about Dollarbill. I showed him the bent spur and told him what had happened. Then I asked, "Mr. Streeter, what do you do about a horse that rolls with the saddle on?"

He thought a moment, then replied, "Take it off."

I nodded.

When he had finished unhitching the trailer, he said, "Let me see that spur." He looked it over, went up to his shop, and after two minutes' work on the anvil, he had hammered it back into perfect shape. Then he said, "Let's go up to the house and put the supper on."

The house was a big square two-story building that sat in a grove of large thrifty trees on a little rise overlooking the river. About a quarter of a mile to the southwest stood Mt. Rochester, the highest of several hills in that vicinity, and about half a mile east of the house was the wide dry bed of Point Creek. The house was built around 1910 by A. H. Tandy, who constructed it of solid concrete blocks that were made on the spot.

Old Tandy was quite a man. In the 1880s he sent cattle up the trail from Haskell, Texas, to the railheads in Kansas. Later, he made and lost several fortunes speculating on land in the Pecos River country of Texas. Around the turn of the century, he moved to Woodward, Indian Territory, built a palatial home, and began buying land in the Texas Panhandle. At that time every other section belonged to the railroad and the rest was state land. Tandy bought only railroad sections, which put his holdings in a checkerboard pattern. Legally, he didn't own any of the land that adjoined him, as those sections belonged to the state and could be sold to anyone who wanted to buy them. But he grazed his land and the state's land too, and if someone was foolish enough to file on the state land, he simply ran them out of the country. One time a man filed on several sections north of the river, right in the middle of Tandy's holdings. Tandy tried repeatedly to buy him out, but he wouldn't sell. So Tandy waited and watched for the proper moment. When the settler made the mistake of butchering a Tandy beef, the old man sent his cowboys out one night to do some persuading. They dragged him out of his cabin in Bourbonese Canyon, tied a rope around his neck, and threw the other end over a tree limb. Then they took out the slack and handed him a paper to sign. When he had signed his holdings over to Tandy, the boys gave him a horse and fifty dollars and told him to leave the country. He left the country.

Another story of Tandy's forceful personality comes out of the Oklahoma Panhandle, where he grazed cattle on land that was unfenced and unsettled. When the country was opened up and settlers began moving in, Tandy did his best to run them out. His cattle knocked down their fences and invaded their fields, and when they retaliated, he filed suit against them and tried to break them in long court battles, which he could afford and they could not.

Finally the settlers brought in big dogs trained to chase cattle. This stratagem worked very well for a while, but Mr. Tandy did not take it lying down. His response was a classic. Though an aggressive man, he gave the appearance of being just the opposite. Soft-spoken and rather frail of body, he struck people who didn't know him as a kind gentleman who might have been a clerk or a bookkeeper. Around sundown he would ride up to a farmer's house and ask for a drink of water. The farmer, who knew Tandy by name only, would go down to the

Jim Streeter rides his horse across the "mighty" Canadian River, which on that particular day was as dry as a sugar bowl.

well to fetch him a dipper of water, never suspecting that this meek gentleman was the notorious Mr. Tandy from the Canadian River. While the host was gone, Tandy would make friends with the dogs that had come up to sniff his legs. Having introduced himself, he would reach into his pocket and come out with strips of poisoned meat, which they would swallow in one gulp. When the farmer returned with the water, he would find the stranger petting the dogs behind the ears. Tandy would drink the water, thank the man, and ride away. Then, a few hours later, the farmer would find three or four dead dogs in his front yard.

Tandy was shrewd, all right. One time he shipped a train-load of cattle to market in Kansas City. On the return trip, he was carrying a large amount of cash in his coat pocket. At some point along the way, he looked out the window and saw several cowboys on horseback riding beside the train. He stood up, yawned, and told his traveling companion he was going to get a drink of water. By the time he had returned from the water cooler, the train had come to a halt. The door burst open and several men with guns entered the car. They ordered the passengers to raise their hands and stand against the wall, while they went through everyone's pockets collecting valuables and money. Very calmly, Tandy surrendered his pocket watch and a few dollars in cash from his wallet. His traveling companion kept waiting for the robbers to find the big roll of bills he had been carrying and was amazed when they left without it. When the bandits had gone, he turned to Tandy and whispered, "What happened to the cattle money?" Tandy smiled and told him to follow. They walked to the water cooler, Tandy removed the lid, and the friend looked in to see five figures worth of cash floating around in the water.

"How did you know they were going to rob the train?" the man asked. "I thought they were just cowboys."

Drying off his money with a towel, Tandy replied, "Every one of those men was riding a horse with a different brand. If they'd been cowboys, the horses would have been branded the same."

In his prime, Mr. Tandy owned a hundred sections of land in Roberts and Ochiltree Counties, and controlled virtually all the country between the river and the headwaters of Wolf Creek, a straight distance of about seventeen miles. He ran his empire from Woodward during the winter and spent the summers on the river. In the early 1900s, at a time when telephones were practically unheard of in Canadian, Miami, and Ochiltree, Tandy installed his own private line between Woodward and the ranch headquarters. (Ironically, sixty years later, Jim Streeter still doesn't have a phone.)

The Tandy Ranch of 1972 was only a small part of the original holdings and belonged to the heirs of Tandy's daughter, Mary Morrison of San Antonio. Jim Streeter operated the ranch for Martin and Scammon, who had it under lease. Streeter came from a long line of cow people. His grandfather, A. J. Streeter, led wagon trains over the Santa Fe Trail, fought Indians, and finally settled down to the more sedentary life of ranch manager in Kansas. A. J.'s son Frank established the Palmia Ranch in southeastern Colorado on the Cimarron River, and it was there that Jim Streeter was born and raised. He cowboyed in the Cimarron country for a number of years, then moved down to the Canadian in 1953.

Over the years he established a solid reputation as a man of integrity, an efficient cow man, and an expert roper. He dressed in modest cowboy style, wearing blue jeans, cowboy boots, and western straw hat that he pulled down almost to the tops of his glasses. Rather quiet and soft-spoken, he laughed easily at the jokes of another man, but dropped his own cracks into the conversation without a smile. His wit was as dry as a sand dune, and occasionally you had to look under the brim of his hat to see if that mischievous little sparkle had come into his eyes. It was the contrast between his mournful, immobile expression and the agile mind at work behind it that made his humor so effective.

And another unusual thing about Jim Streeter. Although he belonged to a profession which had produced some of the most colorful invective in the English language, I never once heard him swear. For this alone his name should go down in the Cowboy Hall of Fame.

As the sun slipped behind Mt. Rochester, we gathered in the kitchen. While Mr. Streeter bent over the stove and stirred the supper, Bill and I sat around the table, smoking and supervising the chef, who we figured needed all the advice he could get. But I'll have to admit the chef did all right. The service could have been improved, but we could find no fault with Mr. Streeter's fried steak, pan fried potatoes, and hot biscuits. My only complaint about the meal came when our host offered me an innocent looking little green pepper from his garden.

119

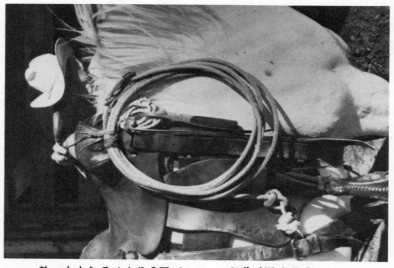

Left: a patient grandfather, Jim Streeter listens as grandson James Ray Morris tells a fish story. James Ray's sister Amy does not appear to have swallowed it hook, line, and sinker.

Right: Streeter saddles up his big white horse. His rigging and equipment indicate that he is accustomed to roping.

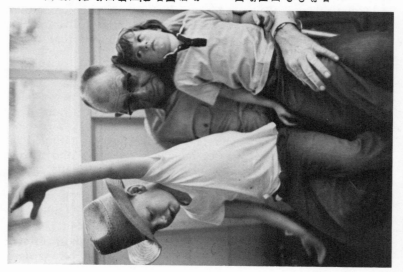

I asked if it was hot. "Not very," he told me. So, like a dope, I took a bite and entertained my companions by breathing flames for about five minutes. Mr. Streeter protested his innocence, but I saw him chuckling behind his biscuit.

When the dishes had been cleared, Mr. Streeter told us the sad tale of a cowboy named Johnny. Streeter knew him when they were both young men in Colorado. Johnny was one of the best bronc riders in that part of the country, and as far as anyone knew, he'd never been bucked off a horse but one time, and that particular horse had been an outlaw that had piled many a good cowboy. Someone once asked him his secret for staying on a bucking horse. "Well sir," he replied, "I try to put a leg on each side and keep my mind in the middle." (I believe that was also Jim Shoulders's formula, though the expression may be older than Johnny or Shoulders.) Johnny was so good that he started riding saddle broncs on the rodeo circuit, joining his father and two brothers. A cousin had also ridden until a horse had fallen on him and left him paralyzed for life.

One day Johnny was riding in a rodeo in Colorado. He stayed with his horse until the whistle blew, then the pickup man rode in and grabbed the rein. But he was on the wrong side, so that when pressure was applied to the rein, it pulled the bronc's head around and up toward the rider, causing him to flip over on his side. Johnny saw it coming and cried, "Don't do it!" But the pickup man didn't hear him or didn't understand, and when he dallied up, the bronc flipped over on Johnny, crushing him.

He lay unconscious in the hospital for a whole month, hovering between life and death. Finally he regained consciousness and began responding to treatment, but he was never the same after the accident. He had trouble getting around, spoke with a slur, and couldn't remember little things like names and dates. And of course he could never ride a horse again.

Jim Streeter, who had moved down to the Canadian country, heard about the accident and the next time he was in Colorado he stopped in to visit his old friend. When Johnny saw him, he squinted his eyes and said, "I remember you. You're from the Cimarron country. I remember your face and I know it well, but I can't call your name." Jim smiled and told him his name, but didn't mention that he'd been away from the Cimarron country for several years. Johnny apologized for not remembering his name and promised he wouldn't forget it again.

And he didn't. The next time they met was at the funeral of a mutual friend. Out at the cemetery the mourners were making their way to the grave to pay their last respects to the deceased. Most walked quietly or spoke in whispers. But when Johnny saw his old friend, he couldn't contain himself. As if to make up for the time before, he blurted out, "Ah, Jimmy, Jimmy!" and came hobbling over to take his hand. He hadn't forgotten.

The last Jim Streeter heard, Johnny was running a little cowboy museum in Colorado and getting by on the nickels and dimes of tourists. Any time Jim ran across an old spur or bridle bit, he boxed it up and sent it to Johnny's museum.

The story put us all in kind of a lonesome mood, and after we had sat around the table thinking of Johnny for a while, Mr. Streeter glanced up at the electric clock on the wall and said maybe it was time to call it a day. At the foot of the stairs, we said good night. Mr. Streeter went up to his room and we filed out to the screened porch, where he had prepared a bed for us. About two minutes after crawling between the sheets, Bill began to snore, and before I had time to wonder if he would keep me awake all night, I awoke, and it was morning.

XVI

Awanyu, Gold and Poor George

As we were cleaning up the breakfast dishes, Floyd Morris came in the back door with his two small children, James Ray and Amy. Streeter's son-in-law, Floyd worked on the Tandy ranch, and he and his family lived in a mobile home about fifty yards south of the house. He and I didn't need to be introduced, as we had attended high school together in Perryton. At a time when the rest of us gave very little thought to the future, Floyd had known exactly what he wanted to do. He wanted to be a cowboy. On graduating from high school, he went straight to the river and hired on with the Brainard outfit. In the ten years since, he had worked the north side of the river all the way from John's Creek to the Oklahoma line.

He said that if we wanted, he would take us around the ranch and show us a couple of spots that might be of interest, so we loaded up in the four-wheel drive and went for a Sunday ride. We were especially interested in locating an Indian rock painting on Mt. Rochester, and that was the first place we went. Working our way up to a shallow cave on the south face, we found the pictograph. Drawn with some sort of orange paint on the protected ceiling of the cave, the image appeared to be a rattlesnake about four feet long, with a long forked tongue protruding from the head.

As far as I know, this site has never been studied or written up by a professional archeologist, so we can only guess at its

123

age and significance. Since the Panhandle Pueblo Indians occupied this section of the river, it is a safe assumption that the artist belonged to this culture. A second line of evidence comes from the fact that these Indians often depicted reptiles in their rock paintings. In the 1931 issue of the *Panhandle-Plains Historical Review*, Floyd Studer wrote:

> One of the important religious symbols of the Pueblo Indian is the plumed serpent, called *Awanyu*. It looks like a reptile, has plumes on his head and body, and was an emblem of mythical power. *Awanyu* conserved water . . . A figure quite like the *Awanyu* is found in the Panhandle (on Rocky Dell Creek in Oldham County).

I have no idea whether or not the pictograph we found on Mt. Rochester belongs to the *Awanyu* class and thus expresses some profound religious feeling in the artist. Maybe it's an *Awanyu* and maybe it's just a snake. Sometimes I can't help smiling at how determined we moderns are at giving somber interpretations to such things. We have reconstructed our ancestors as a rather grim and humorless lot, a civilization of loin-clothed James Joyces who went about scribbling epiphanic messages on slabs of rock. I would just as soon believe that the artist bedded down one night under the rock ledge, awoke the next morning to find a rattlesnake beside him, and, with a shaky hand, drew a warning on the ceiling for the next occupant of the cave. Admittedly, this interpretation excludes the possibility of grand mythological power and dark significance, but it opens up other avenues, such as humor and whimsey.[1]

From this spot near the top of Mt. Rochester, we commanded a stunning view of the Canadian valley. Across the river we could see the timbered outline of three creeks that headed up in the rolling hill country around Miami, fifteen miles to the south. I knew one of them had to be Horse Creek and I got out my map to see which it was. I was especially interested in Horse Creek because I believed an incident occurred there many years ago which historians have not placed in this part of the Panhandle.

The story comes to us through the diary of Josiah Gregg, an early day explorer who led an expedition up the Canadian in 1839. In his entry for June 8, Gregg observes, "It was somewhere in this vicinity that a small party of Americans experienced a terrible calamity in the winter of 1832–3." The party was composed of twelve men, "chiefly citizens of Missouri," who had completed a successful year of trading around Santa Fe. As winter approached, they prepared to make the long trip back to Missouri, then the western edge of the frontier. The safest and most commonly followed route, the Cimarron Cutoff of the Santa Fe Trail, would have taken them through Kansas and on into Missouri, but since they were getting a late start, they elected to follow the Canadian River instead. The Canadian route was not only more direct, but also several hundred miles south of the Santa Fe Trail and less likely to be clogged with snow.

The party left Santa Fe in December with ten thousand dollars in gold specie loaded on pack animals and enough saddle horses to make the seven-hundred-mile trip. One morning, after they had been on the trail for several weeks, they observed a party of Kiowa and Comanche warriors up ahead, and before they knew it the Indians had them completely surrounded. They didn't panic, but neither did they intend to stop when the Indians made signs for them to dismount. Getting their guns ready for quick use, they tried to ride through the warriors. Then a rifle cracked and a man named Pratt fell dead to the ground, and the battle began. The others dismounted and began returning the fire. Mitchell, another trader, was killed.

The traders laid down a deadly fire while they took the packs and saddles off the animals and threw up a breastworks. The Indians launched several charges but were beaten back by superior firepower. Before long the traders had entrenched themselves behind the breastworks and established a strong defensive position. Seeing this, the Indians changed their strategy. Instead of making reckless charges, they held back in the distance and put their sharpshooters to work. "In a few hours," Gregg writes, "all the animals of the traders were either killed or wounded."

The merchants probably hoped the Indians would tire of a long siege and finally give it up, but the Indians proved very stubborn and refused to leave. The battle dragged on for thirty-six hours, and although the traders had plenty of dead horses to eat, they were cut off from water. During the night they held a conference and decided they would either escape now or perish from thirst. Since they would have to make their escape on foot, each man took only the amount of gold he could safely carry. "In this way a few hundred dollars were started with, of which,

Left: James Ray Morris checks out a hole in the rocks.

Right: Amy Morris enjoys the view of the river valley from a shallow cave, while looking for the Indian petroglyph on Mt. Rochester.

however, but little ever reached the United States. The remainder was buried deep in the sand, in hopes that it might escape the cupidity of the savages."

And so the ten remaining traders slipped off into the night and began their journey back to civilization. Without provisions or ammunition for hunting, they lived on roots and bark. When an argument arose over the best route back, they split up into two parties of five. One of these parties eventually reached the Creek settlements on the Arkansas River, but in the other party only two survived.

Gregg's journal is very vague as to the exact location of the attack, but I think we can forgive him for this, since he didn't know exactly where *he* was most of the time, let alone where the traders had met their fate. In *The XIT Ranch of Texas*, J. Evetts Haley places the attack "in the Western Panhandle." I think it might have taken place on Horse Creek in Roberts County.²

In the fall of 1971 I spent an afternoon talking with H. L. Ledrick, Jr., whose people settled on Chicken Creek in the 1880s. Among other things, I asked him how the creeks on the south side of the river had gotten their names. When we came to Horse Creek, he scratched his head and said he didn't know. Then he thought about it for a moment and said he did remember one thing his father had told him. He had said that when the country was first settled, the mouth of this creek had been covered with horse bones, lots of them. During hard times, the ranchers had loaded the bones in wagons and sold them to a fertilizer company. And, he supposed, that was how Horse Creek got its name. Where had all the bones come from? Could he explain why so many horses had died in this one spot? No, he couldn't.

Of course the fact that there were a large number of horse bones at the mouth of the creek does not prove that the horses belonged to the Santa Fe traders, but it's not a bad guess either. Why would a large number of horses die in the same spot? They were not killed for food or hides by either the Indians or the hunters, both of whom needed saddle horses and beasts of burden and could count on an abundant supply of meat from other sources. The bones could have come from a herd of wild horses that died in a blizzard, but it seems unlikely that a breed of animals as hardy as the mustangs, who had spent generations on the Plains, would perish in a storm the way imported cattle

Floyd Morris, Jim Streeter's son-in-law, who worked as a cowboy on the Tandy Ranch.

did. In 1972 I presented this line of reasoning to J. Evetts Haley and asked his opinion. He shrugged and said, "Sure could be."

＊　＊　＊

From Mt. Rochester Floyd drove us up into Bourbonese Canyon, and around noon we arrived back at the house. Mr. Streeter had a big pot of red beans bubbling on the stove, and after lunch we sat around talking about horses and cattle and people we knew on the river. Then the conversation took a depressing turn, as Bill and I remembered that tomorrow morning we would hit the trail again with our old friend, Dobbin Mule. With the memory of Saturday's miseries still vivid in our minds, we discussed ways of getting more speed out of the mule, none of which seemed very convincing. Then Mr. Streeter said, "Well, if you boys want to take him back to Wolf Creek, I'll be glad to loan you a pickup." Our spirits rose tremendously on those words, as once again Mr. Streeter had managed to read our most secret thoughts. Bill needed to go into Perryton to buy more film anyhow, and it wouldn't be much out of his way to drop the mule off at the Herndon ranch on Wolf Creek.

We brought our camping gear up from the saddlehouse and began cutting it down to what we could carry with us on the horses: a slicker and bedroll apiece, plus enough jerky, rice, and raisins to keep us alive for the remainder of the trip. Then we loaded Dobbin in the pickup and Bill hauled him back home.

After they had gone, Mr. Streeter stretched out in the living room for an afternoon nap and I went out on the back porch to catch up on my journal entries. It was quiet and peaceful out there, the air still and fragrant. For a while I watched a mother swallow leaning over her mud nest under the eaves, then I opened my notebook and brought it up to date. When Mr. Streeter got up from his nap, we walked down to the corrals to check the horses. While we were there he pointed to a charred post in the corral fence and told me how it had gotten that way.

One night a few years ago a thunderstorm moved in from the north. Lightning flashed across the sky and thunder exploded like bombshells. One of the Streeter girls was afraid of storms and couldn't sleep, so she happened to be awake when a bolt of lightning struck the barn. Looking out, she saw that it had started a fire and she ran upstairs to tell her father. Streeter looked out the window, grabbed his clothes and ran down the stairs, dressing as he went.

There were two horses in the corral. One of them was his favorite saddlehorse which he had raised from a colt.

By the time he reached the lot, a strong north wind was fanning the blaze that had grown into a raging inferno, blowing the flames directly into the pen where the horses were. He threw open the gate to let them out, but by this time they had gone crazy with fear and were dashing from one end of the corral to the other. Streeter ran across the lot, almost roasting in the intense heat, and managed to run one of them out the gate. Then he tried to get the other, his favorite, to follow. But the horse had lost his head, and suddenly he bolted around the lot one last time and ran straight into the burning barn.

I can't say how Mr. Streeter felt that night, but as he told me the story, probably ten or fifteen years later, I honestly believe he felt pain. When I asked a question or two about the fire, he became evasive and changed the subject.

When Bill returned late that afternoon, Mr. Streeter took us for a ride up into Wright Canyon to show us where he had found pieces of a still. Up near the head, the canyon forked. We got out of the pickup and followed a heavily timbered draw that ran into the west fork. Near a seep spring shaded by very tall cedar trees, we found a rusted barrel hoop. A short distance away, we found two sunken spots in the ground where dugouts had once stood. Someone had operated here, all right, and I was betting this was the place where Ben Hill and his brother found the dead possums in Choctaw Slim's water hole. As we drove back to the house, we looked back and saw a big anvil-shaped thundercloud in the northern sky. Bathed in pastel pinks and violets of sundown, it towered seven or eight miles above the prairie, while the rest of the country disappeared into the shadows of evening.

It was dark by the time we sat down to a supper of red beans and cornbread. Mr. Streeter apologized for serving the same entree twice in a row, but then put his apology into perspective by adding, "But I don't know why a person would want anything else." Our mouths stuffed, Bill and I could only nod our agreement. After the meal Bill and I cleaned up the kitchen. Mr. Streeter, fresh from his afternoon nap, was in an impish mood and told us one of his best yarns.

130

One summer a crew moved onto the Tandy ranch to cut and bale prairie hay in the meadow pastures. The Streeters fixed up the spare bedrooms and told the crew they could stay there while they were on the ranch. Now, one of these men— I'll call him George—had a problem. He walked in his sleep. He explained to the Streeters that it wasn't unusual for him to walk around the house at night or even to wander outside, so if they heard someone prowling around in the middle of the night they shouldn't be surprised or frightened.

That night Streeter awoke with an unusual feeling. He sat up in bed and cocked his ear. Off in another part of the house, he heard a strange noise, a kind of grunting and moaning. Creeping through the darkness, he followed the sound to the bathroom, where he discovered George behind the door. He had somnambulated into the bathroom to answer nature's call, but he had tried to exit on the wrong side of the door. Streeter took him by the hand and led him back to bed.

The next day Jim spread the story around and rode George high all day long. George was properly embarrassed, but there wasn't much he could say.

Well, the next day Mrs. Streeter gathered the laundry out of the dirty clothes hamper in the bathroom and began her regular weekly wash. Seeing this, Jim hatched a demonic plan. When George came into the kitchen for breakfast, Jim was waiting like a hungry coyote on a rabbit trail. With a ver-ry serious expression on his face—and no one could do it better or more convincingly than he—he took George to the back door and pointed to Mrs. Streeter, who was hanging the wash out on the line.

"George," he said, shaking his head, "I hate to tell you this."

George, as innocent as the rabbit in whose role he had been cast, frowned and drew closer. "What, Jim? What's the matter?"

Streeter furrowed his brow and sighed. "George, I . . . maybe I shouldn't say anything about this, but . . ."

"About what?" He was getting worried.

"But I thought you might want to know."

"Know *what?* What's wrong, Jim? Good lord, it must be terrible."

Streeter arched his brows. "Yeah, I'm afraid it's bad news. George," he looked him straight in the eye, "you walked in your sleep again last night."

He sighed. "Oh me. What did I do, Jim? Go on, tell me. Don't hold anything back."

Jim lowered his voice. "You peed in the laundry basket."

"Oh no! Oh lord no, Jim! I . . . oh good lord! No, I couldn't have, Jim."

"Yeah, well," he examined his fingernails, "my wife didn't want to say anything about it. You know, she just took the laundry out and washed it early this morning and . . ."

George turned and banged his head against the wall. "Oh Jim, this is too embarrassing for words! Look, I've never done anything like this before. I swear I haven't."

"Uh huh."

"Are you sure? Are you dead sure certain?"

Streeter shrugged. "Well, let's go up to the bathroom and see what we can find."

George took this to be a fair test. What he didn't know was that there just happened to be a big brown water stain on the bathroom wall, and it just happened to be directly behind the laundry basket. Streeter pulled back the hamper and pointed to the stain. "What's *that*?"

George closed his eyes on this damning evidence and moaned, "Oh no! How could I!"

Jim patted him on the shoulder. "I'm sorry, George. But don't worry about it. We can get the wall repapered."

George was mortified. "Jim, how can I ever face Mrs. Streeter again?"

"I don't know, George. It'll be hard. But I can tell you that she'll never mention it." This seemed to comfort him a bit, but as Streeter turned and walked away, he added, "To you, anyway."

Chuckling over the story of Poor George, we said good night to our host and retired to our bed on the porch. As usual, Bill dropped right off to sleep and began his nightly imitation of a Diesel truck. I couldn't sleep, but it wasn't Bill that kept me awake. An image had begun to glow in the back of my mind: I could almost see Jim Streeter lying in his bed and grinning in the darkness, as he sorted through his repertoire of pranks, searching for the one that would be just right for Bill and me.

XVII

Bar CC Ranch and Dave Lard

The next morning, over fried ham, biscuits, and gravy, we began asking Mr. Streeter for information about the river bottom. Although we had been "on the river" for a week, we had yet to cross it or even to get within a quarter mile of the stream bed. This morning we would cross over to the south bank for the first time, and we wanted to know what to expect in the way of quicksand.

The rivers of the Plains, including the Cimarron, the Beaver, and the various forks of the Red, as well as the Canadian, have always been a natural barrier to travel. In the rainy season a horseman might find the river running bank-to-bank with water, in which case he would either have to swim his horse across or wait for the water to recede. But then he might find crossing even more of a hazard, as by then the river bed would have become boggy with quicksand. There is nothing particularly exotic about quicksand. It is nothing more than common sand that has become highly saturated with water, and it presents more danger to livestock than to humans. Cattle and horses are heavy enough to sink into the bogs, and if they are not pulled out they can die from starvation and exposure. We had never heard a reliable report of a person being swallowed up on the river, but we did not wish to become the first victims.

Mr. Streeter was rather vague in responding to our questions, then casually mentioned that he had to go check some cattle out in the river pasture anyway, so he'd escort us across. I really doubt that he had anything that needed checking on the river, but we were glad that we would be making our first river crossing under the experienced eye of Jim Streeter.

After breakfast, we went down to the pens and worked out a way of carrying our gear, now that we no longer had the services of Dobbin. We rolled our bedding and slickers in a tight roll, placed them behind the cantle of the saddle, and lashed them down with saddle strings. The rest of the gear we put in makeshift saddlebags, consisting of two canvas bags tied together with a leather thong and strapped down behind our bedrolls. Then we led the horses out of the lot and headed toward the river.

The river turned out to be quite a disappointment. After wading a little slue on the north bank, we didn't see another drop of water. The old riverbed measured about a quarter mile across at this point and had grown up in salt cedar and brush. The stream bed was divided into two channels, but we found no water in either, and no evidence of quicksand. On reaching the cutbank on the south side, Mr. Streeter pointed the way to the McMordie headquarters, gave us his hand, and wished us good luck. Then he turned back across the river, and we rode on to the south. When we parted with Jim Streeter, I felt as though I were saying good-bye to a favorite uncle.

From the south bank it was only a two-mile ride to the McMordie ranch, which we made with only one incident worth telling. As we were trotting along, we rode upon a wild turkey sitting on a nest. Bill saw her just before she flew and gave us just enough warning to "choke horn and claw leather." Suds and Dollarbill both jumped about ten feet to the west, but this time we managed to keep a leg on each side and our minds in the middle.

The Frank McMordie ranch was operated by a young man of twenty-eight named David Trimble. As we rode up, we found him unloading block salt at the barn. After we had put up the horses, David said he had something we might be interested in seeing. We followed him around to the south side of the house, where he called, "Here Antelope! Heeeeere Antelope!" An instant later a spindly-legged raisin-eyed little creature came bounding around the side of the house and began nursing one of David's fingers. A week before, some men had spotted a baby antelope alone in a pasture. Thinking the mother would return to claim it,

134

David Trimble, cowboy on the McMordie Ranch, offers a drink to his pet antelope.

they went on. But they returned around dusk just to be sure, and finding the baby still alone, they caught it and dropped it off at David Trimble's place. Had they not done so, the antelope would almost certainly have been eaten by coyotes. David and his family had been feeding it on a bottle for about two weeks and the little dickens had become as tame as a puppy. It came at a call and followed its new family everywhere they went. One of David's sisters had tried to give it a proper name—Brandy—but it appeared that after two weeks, Antelope, or Ann, had become the common usage.

Our primary interest on the McMordie ranch was the ruins of the old Bar CC Ranch headquarters. Established in 1876 with headquarters on Home Ranch Creek, the Bar CC controlled some twelve hundred square miles of open range, and ran as many as thirty thousand head of cattle. When the ranch terminated its operations in 1886, many of the cowboys stayed in the country and established smaller operations of their own. Among them were E. H. Brainard, Archie King, and Dave Lard.

Dave Lard. Now there's a man who left behind some tales. In 1889 when rival factions in Roberts County almost went to war over the location of the county seat, Dave Lard, a powerful, quick-tempered cowboy, took an active part. At one point the county had two complete sets of officers and neither admitted the legitimacy of the other. When the officers of the rival faction refused to answer a court call in Lipscomb County, Dave Lard took the matter into his own hands. After having been deputized by the sheriff of his faction, Lard rode into Miami, kidnapped the other side's sheriff, county judge, and county clerk, handcuffed them to seats on the eastbound train, and shipped them off to Canadian.

Bill Lard of Miami told me another story on his kinsman. Back in 1905 a man named Tom Stewart was sheriff of Roberts County. Stewart had a bad temper and a mean disposition, and he made a habit of taking his temper out on the kids. Many people considered him overbearing and looked forward to the day when he took his meanness out on the wrong people.

That occasion arose when he arrested several of Dave Lard's nephews on some minor offense. Now, the Lard boys weren't bad; they just enjoyed a good time. I don't know what law they had broken on this occasion, but the county court records for subsequent years might provide some indication:

136

With the river valley still shrouded in early morning haze, David Trimble brings Suds and Dollarbill up from the pasture.

1909—W. S. Lard, swearing and cursing in public
1913—J. D. Lard, betting on the outcome of a local election
1913—Willie Lard, gaming at the Cap Rock Hotel
1914—Roy Lard, gaming
1917—Claude Lard, gaming
1923—Bill Lard, drunkenness

In any case, Dave felt injustice had been done. When he heard that Sheriff Stewart had arrested his nephews, he stormed over to the courthouse in Miami and met Stewart on the front steps. Lard wanted to know what was going on, and Stewart told him to mind his own business. As they faced each other, tempers flared and voices rose.

Now, Dave was a big strong man. He packed a wicked left-hand wallop and had been known to use it on several occasions. When he had taken all he could of Sheriff Stewart, he lost his temper and swung. The left caught Stewart squarely in the face, and it was delivered with such force that it knocked one of his eyeballs out of his head and left it hanging on his cheek. Wounded and horrified, Stewart drew his pistol and shot Dave, who fell to the courthouse steps.

Stewart thought he had killed him, when in fact he had only shot him through the thigh. But he didn't wait around to find out. By then he could think of only two things: the grotesque condition of his face and the swift revenge of Dave Lard's family. He ran through town, down to the railroad tracks where he met one of his own deputies. The deputy had heard the shot and asked what was going on.

"Keep away from me!" Stewart replied, covering his eye and backing away like a wounded animal. "Just keep away from me!" The deputy saw that Stewart was desperate, and he went back to the courthouse.

Stewart followed the railroad tracks to his house, which stood just north of the depot. His wife had been baking all afternoon and had just set five fruit pies out on the table to cool. All at once the kitchen door burst open and in walked her husband, his eyeball hanging out on his cheek.

"My God, Tom, what's happened to you!" she cried.

"I've just killed Dave Lard," he said, staring at her with his one good eye. "Go down to the depot and wire Rube Hutton in Dalhart. Tell him what's happened."

For a moment the woman stood speechless. "But Tom, what about . . . your *eye!*"

"Never mind about my eye!" he shouted. "Do as I said. Get out! Get out! *Get out!*"

The poor woman must have been terrified. Snatching up her bonnet, she fled from the house. When she had gone, Stewart stood there for a long time, trying to think through the situation. He had lost an eye. He had just killed one of the most prominent ranchers in Roberts County. And by this time the word would have gotten out, and somewhere in the darkness the Lards, who had never liked him anyway, were coming to get him. He didn't want to die by their guns, nor did he want to have their blood on his conscience. In this desperate state of mind, he could think of only one solution.

He cocked his pistol, put it to his temple, and blew his brains out.

Bill Hardin of Canadian was just a small boy at that time and happened to be one of the first to arrive at the scene. It is very strange the things children see and remember. Hardin had no memory of the body, the pistol, or the dead man's face. All he could remember of that night was staring at those nice fresh pies on the table, all ruined with blood and brains.

Dave Lard recovered from the leg wound and lived to a ripe old age. As he got up in years, it became harder and harder for him to get around. All the broken bones and bullet holes of his youth began to ache. The body that had once been heavy with muscles went soft and he developed into rather a fat man. And then to make matters worse, he was cursed with a grouchy prostate that dealt him no end of misery. He became so crippled up, in fact, that whenever he went some place, his wife had to go along. As inconspicuously as possible, she would hook her finger in one of his belt loops and support him as he hobbled around.

But if time had softened Dave Lard's body, it had failed to mellow his temperament. Indeed, all his physical miseries made old Dave even more cantankerous and ill-tempered than ever. Dave always enjoyed baseball, and in his old age he attended baseball games in Pampa every time he got the chance. To these games he always went in the company of his faithful wife, finger-in-loop, and a man named Gilmer, who ran the movie house in Pampa. Lard had his troubles, but so did Gilmer, who had been dismembered in a terrible accident that had left him with two hooks and a peg leg. Besides his disability, Gilmer had several other qualities in common with

139

old Dave: both men loved baseball, both had strong opinions and tempers to match, and both were prone to fight when their tempers were aroused.

The story goes that Gilmer and Lard went to a baseball game in Pampa. They got into a discussion about a rule or bit of baseball history. The discussion became an argument. Both men were yelling. And then would you believe it, these two old invalids got into a fist-and-hook fight in the stands!

✿ ✿ ✿

I didn't know where the old Bar CC headquarters was located, or if it could even be found anymore. David Trimble wasn't sure either, but as we talked about it he remembered riding over some kind of ruins off in the pasture. So after a meal of Mrs. Trimble's fried steak, we climbed into the pickup and headed south. About seven miles up Home Ranch Creek, we located the spot.

Not much was left to see of the house, just a vague outline with a porch foundation made of rock and cedar timbers buried in the ground. Scattered about on the ground we found square nails, pieces of glass and crockery, and some chunks of iron that might have come from a cook stove. About fifty yards northwest of the house, we located a set of wire corrals with two pens. The pen on the north was dug into the side of a hill and I would guess that poles were laid across the top to form a shelter from winter storms. We found two kinds of wire on the posts, the common Glidden barb and a hog wire with diamond-shaped mesh. Between the house and the pens we came across an old well which had almost completely filled with dirt.

In 1882 the Bar CC Ranch moved its headquarters from Home Ranch Creek up to Wolf Creek in Ochiltree County. The day before, Bill Ellzey had driven right past the site of the Wolf Creek headquarters when he had taken Dobbin back to the Herndon ranch. The site now lies on the Herndon ranch, and for all we knew, at that moment Dobbin the Mule was cropping grass on the very spot where old Dave Lard had once eaten his meals.

XVIII

Horseshoes with Ben Hill

The next morning David Trimble rode down to the river with us and showed us the best place to cross. Our second crossing was as uneventful as the first, and again we found the river dry except for a few slues and pools.

Our destination this day was the Ben Hill ranch on Barton Creek, a short ride of about four miles. Ben Hill's son Arnold lived on the place then, having recently returned from a fifteen-year stay in California, where he worked as a stuntman in motion pictures and television. He and his wife Alice lived in a mobile home about half a mile west of the corrals and bunkhouse. Alice, a California woman, seemed to have adapted well to living on the prairie and spoke of how pleasant it was to be able to breathe fresh air.

We found Arnold, Ben, and Ben's grandson, J. C. Hill, at the bunkhouse talking over the day's work schedule. After they showed us where to put the horses, the Hills held a short caucus and decided that since company had arrived on the ranch, they would postpone the work until after lunch. J. C. was dispatched to the bunkhouse to put the meal on the stove, while the rest of us went down to a grove of trees to pitch horseshoes.

After lunch, Mr. Hill washed the dishes while Arnold and the rest of us drove out into the pasture to locate a herd of steers. During the meal there had been some talk of moving the steers down to a pasture along the river, and Arnold had

141

Ben Hill, long-time rancher in the Canadian river valley, takes aim with a horseshoe. Ordinarily a kind and gentle man, he showed his guests no mercy at the horseshoe pits.

thought it would be a good idea to find out where they were before we set out on horseback. We returned with a gloomy report: the cattle were badly scattered and had gone into the brush to find some shade. Furthermore, it was bloody hot. Over glasses of tea, Arnold and Mr. Hill weighed the need to move the cattle against the inconvenience of doing it against the fact that what everybody really wanted to do was pitch horseshoes in the shade. Mr. Hill heard all the evidence, pondered for a minute or two, and ruled in favor of horseshoes. We retired to the pits.

Ben Hill had been on the river since the 1920s. He was a kind old gentleman with hazy blue eyes and two hedges of white hair on the sides of his head. Wearing his old slouch hat, he reminded me of Walter Brennan. He was a wicked horseshoe pitcher. Holding the shoe on the right side and throwing for a full turn to the right, he wiped out the younger generation for several hours.

In the middle of the afternoon, we called a recess and went up to the bunkhouse for some more iced tea. As we sat out on the screened porch, Arnold told us about his career in Hollywood. Raised on the Barton Creek ranch, he rode bulls on the professional rodeo circuit for several years and happened to be in California at a time when stuntmen were in demand. During his fifteen years in Hollywood, he stunted in "Gunsmoke," "Rawhide," doubled for Paul Newman in "Hud," and worked in several of the Disney productions. His work included chase scenes, fights, horse falls, and wagon wrecks, mostly western.

A member of the Wrangler's Union, Local 399, he said that every time an animal appeared in a motion picture it had to be accompanied by a wrangler. "If they don't use but one chicken in the whole picture, that chicken has to have a wrangler with him," he told us. He also pointed out that every time an animal was used in a film, a representative from the Humane Society had to be present to see that the animal was not abused.

Arnold left Hollywood when movie makers found that they could make films cheaper outside the United States and moved practically all their locations to Mexico and Europe. Unless a stuntman was willing and able to spend a lot of time away from home, he couldn't find enough work to support himself.

Around sundown, Mr. Hill and J. C. loaded up and went back to Canadian. Arnold returned to his house, and Bill and I retired to the bunkhouse to fix ourselves some supper. This old bunkhouse was a two-room affair without running water or plumbing. We got our water from a twenty-gallon cooler in the kitchen and answered the calls of nature outside. The east room of the bunkhouse doubled as a bedroom and dining room and was furnished with two old poster beds, a dresser, a couple of small couches, and a dining table. The plywood walls were decorated with a Franklin vaccine calendar and two fly swatters, one of the old wire mesh variety, bloodied by many years of service, and the other a newer model of bright yellow plastic. On the west wall of the kitchen hung a large square-faced electric clock advertising Nu-Grape.

After a meal of jerky and rice, we washed up the dishes, pitched the water out, and went to bed. Before turning out the light, we spread our map over the bed and studied the route we would take tomorrow. We planned to cover thirty miles from the Hill place to the Tom Conatser ranch near Lake Marvin. It would be a long hard ride, and if we had still had the mule, we could not have made it in one day.

XIX

Lavender Cowboys
at Springer's Ranch

He was only a lavender cowboy,
The hairs on his chest were two.
He wanted to follow the heroes
To do as the he-men do.

Herpicide and many hair tonics
He rubbed in morning and night,
But when he looked into the mirror,
No new hairs grew in sight.
                    —"The Lavender Cowboy"

At five a.m. we were jarred out of bed by the alarm clock
and staggered to our morning chores. Bill went down to the
corral to give the horses some oats, and I put the breakfast
on to cook.

We left the Hill place around six-thirty. The air was cool
and damp and the valley lay blue and silent around us. About
a mile south, we struck the river road and turned east, just
as a big orange lollypop sun appeared over the tops of the trees.
Trotting the horses, we made good time. About eight miles east
of the Hill ranch, we hit Highway 83 and rode the ditches
another seven or eight miles to the Oasis Truck Stop on the
Higgins highway, just north of Canadian. It was about noon
when we got there, so we stopped and lunched on a Coke and
a candy bar. When we stepped back into the saddle, we began

The author performed dismally on the bucking barrel and acquired some painful education in rodeo riding. However, the Lavender Cowboys enjoyed it immensely.

to feel the heat. We had used up the best part of the day and the second leg of the trip would not be as pleasant as the first.

From the truck stop, we rode south a few hundred yards and turned back east on 2266, a farm-to-market road, which would take us all the way to Lake Marvin. As the afternoon set in, our conversation fell off to the bare minimum of grunting necessary to conduct our business, and for the next four and a half hours we amused ourselves by reading "Please Do Not Litter" on all the litter in the bar ditch.

East of the Ben Hill ranch, the country began to change. The steep caprocks and canyons gave way to rolling sand hills north of the river and tight-land prairies on the south, and the valley widened out into something nearer a saucer than a bowl. The closer we got to Lake Marvin the more wooded the country became, with shinnery, persimmon trees, chinaberry groves, and tall cottonwoods draped with climbing vines. The Conatser ranch was headquartered just east of Boggy Creek, an active stream of water that supplied Lake Marvin and also Lake Kiowa above it.

We reached the Conatser ranch around four-thirty that afternoon and turned the horses out in a little trap, left them with plenty of oats and water, and went looking for Mr. Conatser. He wasn't at the ranch that day, but we found his hired hands, Walter Hand and Shafer Baxter, two high school boys who were living on the place for the summer. Walter was a short stocky kid of about seventeen, with a soft child's face and a pair of dark brooding eyes. Shafer, a blond who smiled easily, was younger and taller than his companion. It was apparent that both of them had devoted a good deal of time that summer to the study of cowboy choreography, as they had acquired the swagger and mannerisms that Puncher had so admired.

That evening they took us for a ride around the ranch, showing us some deer in the meadow pastures, the drilling rig down by the river, the corrals, and Lake Marvin. By this time they had warmed to us, and we talked and teased and had a good time. When we got back to the house, it was dark and the fireflies had come out along Boggy Creek.

In watching these two kids, I wondered how similar they were to the cowboys of another time and generation. It seemed to me there was something distinctly nineteenth century about them. Like most teenagers, their knowledge of the past was only about five years deep, but unlike most they were unconsciously following patterns that had been around for as long as cowboys had been living on Boggy Creek.

Let's take a closer look at Walter as he comes into the house that evening. Once inside, he walks directly into the kitchen and snaps on the radio. In a moment the house is filled with the rhythms and laments of country-western singers. He doesn't have to adjust the dial, for once he had found the best country music station at the beginning of the summer, he had no reason to change it. The rest of what comes over the air waves, the network news and the city-born rock music, he considers junk.

Next, he hangs his hat on the hat rack on the back porch. He has spent some time cultivating this hat and you can tell he is proud of it. It is a black felt with a square crease in the crown and a modest brim. He has done nothing to change the basic shape, but has decorated it with ear tags, vaccinating needles, bullet holes, feathers, and bobby pins.

Walter tells you that he rode a bull in last year's junior rodeo, rode him all the way to the whistle. He brings out a small traveling bag and shows you his bull rope and riding spurs. Then he recreates the ride, describing the bull, the way he came out of the chute, which way he turned, and how he spun. As he talks he tucks his tee shirt into his jeans so you can see that he is wearing a rodeo prize buckle on his belt. You make the mistake of asking, "Did you win that buckle?" He digs his hands into his pockets and frowns. Naw, they was sposed to give him a buckle, but somebody flubbed up and didn't get the buckles ordered and they had to give him cash instead. He's wearing a buckle his brother won a couple of years ago, and he thinks he's entitled to wear it.

Next, he goes into the ice box, gets a bottle of soda pop, and returns to the back porch. He casually pries the bottle cap off with his teeth and spits it on the floor. Then he darts his eyes around the room to make sure that everyone noticed. A little later, he loads his lower lip with Copenhagen snuff, offers everyone in the room a dip, and seems pleased that no one else is man enough to take it on. After he has worked on the snuff for ten or fifteen minutes (and has gone to the back door to spit ten or fifteen times), he shakes a cigarette out of a pack of Camels. Walter scorns filters and smokes Camels on principle. If anyone offers him a Kent or a True, he turns it down with an air of disdain. A Winston or a Marlboro he will accept, though

Lavender Cowboys Shafer Baxter (left) and Walter Hand were working on the Tom Conatser ranch during the summer of 1972.

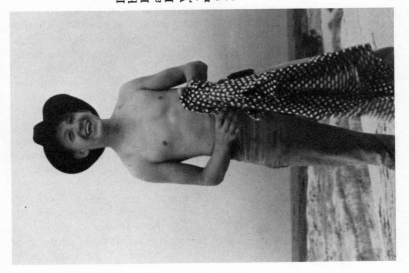

he won't smoke it until he rips off the filter. Although he doesn't smoke more than three or four cigarettes a day, he has affected a smoker's cough to emphasize his nasty habit.

With the Camel dangling from one side of his mouth, he strikes a kitchen match on his front teeth and waits for someone to tell him that you're not supposed to strike matches on your teeth. If you watch closely, you'll notice that he doesn't inhale the smoke, but he's very busy with the cigarette. He holds it *just so* between his thumb and forefinger, rolling it back and forth and constantly flicking the ashes on the floor. Then he stabs it under his lip, lets it hang there while he cocks his head to the side and squints his eyes against the smoke.

Later, he goes into the living room to call his girlfriend. Before he dials the number, he takes her picture out of his billfold and carefully sets it in front of him. They talk for about twenty minutes. He begins by asking her how she's been, allots her about two minutes for her report, then begins talking about his own wicked life. He hasn't had any beer all week, he says, and he's about to die of thirst. Well no, that isn't entirely true since he did get terrible drunk last Saturday. But anyway, he intends to do some serious drinkin' this Saturday night at the dance following the rodeo. Would she care to go with him?

Bill and I bedded down on the screened back porch, while the boys roughed it, setting up cots in the back yard. (A little pre-dawn shower would later send them scurrying back to their warm beds in the house.) We awakened that morning to the patter of soft rain on the giant old cottonwood in the back yard, and to the gobble of wild turkeys that couldn't have been more than thirty yards away.

That afternoon the clouds rolled off to the north and the sun peeked out for the first time. The boys were feeling their oats by then and suggested we all go down and log some time on the bucking barrel. Their bucking barrel consisted of a fifty gallon drum suspended by cables from two trees. While one man sat astride the barrel, the other pulled and pushed on the cables, causing the device to "buck." The bucking barrel is standard equipment for aspiring rodeo riders, who can practice timing and balance without being trampled and gored. The boys covered the barrel with an old strip of carpet, Walter brought out his bull rope, and they showed us how it was done.

It was inevitable that our immunity as visitors would run out, and it wasn't long until the boys tired of dumping each

150

other on the ground and began looking for fresh meat. "Now it's yall's turn," said the boys, who didn't appear quite as innocent as they had the night before. Bill Ellzey was taking pictures at the moment, so I stepped forward, confident that I would get creamed. Since I had never ridden either a bull or a bucking barrel, the boys had to show me how to "screw down." You pass your hand through the loop in the bull rope, wrap the loose end around your palm, clamp down tight, and sit on your hand. The rope felt good and tight in my hand. It was only later that Bill told me these prairie innocents had instructed me in what is known in rodeo circles as the "suicide knot." That extra wrap around the palm gives you a good firm grip on the rope, and you will live happily ever after just as long as you don't get bucked off. But if you *do* get bucked off, you can kiss your arm good-bye at the shoulder because it then becomes the property of the bull.

Sitting atop the barrel, I perceived that the earth was much farther away than I had supposed, there being an empty space of seven feet between eye level and ground level. I also perceived the look of the devil on the faces of the lavender cowboys as they winked and sneered and giggled over the prospect of my taking a dive. I did manage to beg and scold them into allowing me a slow start so that I could get a feel for the barrel. This they granted, not out of any charity but for the same reason a hunter allows his bird to fly. It has nothing to do with the bird, who will be just as dead on the wing as on the ground, but it makes the game more interesting for the hunter. So, with one boy on the front cable and one on the back, they began rocking the barrel.

What I learned in my pre-ride warmup was the basic elementary technique of bronc, bull, and barrel riding. When the rear goes up, you lean back. When the front goes up, you lean forward. You respond to a southward roll with a northward lean, and to a northward roll with a southward lean. The way they got me off was very simple. Just as I had learned to lean north into a southward roll, they gave me two southward rolls and caught me pointing like a birddog toward the north. Then with glee, they tugged and jerked and sent me flying over the side, with my hand still attached to that hangman's knot they had rigged. Between giggles, they wondered if I was all right. Yes, I would be fine, just as soon as I could reunite the ball and socket in my shoulder.

Bill Ellzey enjoyed the same fate, although he didn't allow them to lynch his hand as I had done. At the end of the rodeo, we had compiled a dismal record. We did, however, manage one small triumph. Once when Walter was climbing up onto the barrel, I flipped a head of sand burs onto the seat of his pants. Many laughs when he went down to take a deep seat.

The next morning Mr. Conatser came out after breakfast and we had a chance to sit down and talk. At seventy-three, he was a handsome gentleman with a strong body, a good crop of straight gray hair, and a pair of dancing blue eyes. Several weeks before, I had met him at the Vic Mon Restaurant in Canadian and told him about our proposed trip down the river. He had gotten so excited he could hardly sit still. "That's fine, that's fine!" he had yelled in that distinctive voice of his which acquired volume and exclamation marks the more excited he became. "And you boys stop at my place and stay as long as you want!"

In the cool of morning we went out on the west porch and talked about the history of the Boggy Creek country. The best-known story to come out of Mr. Conatser's piece of the world centered around a man named A. J. Springer. History records that Charles Goodnight and T. S. Bugbee were the first cattle-men to come into the Panhandle in 1876, but actually Springer was there first. In the fall of 1875 he drove three hundred head of cattle into the Boggy Creek country, a full year ahead of Bugbee and Goodnight. He had come to the Canadian valley even earlier than 1875 and had established a trading post and stockade. The trading post, known as Springer's Ranch, carried hunter's supplies which were traded for buffalo hides. The stockade consisted of a blockhouse which was deeply trenched inside and connected to the trading post and corral through underground passages. As John Cook, a buffalo hunter, later described it, "The place was impregnable."

We don't know much about Springer, as he kept mostly to himself and wasn't given to fraternizing with the ranchers and cowboys who came into the country in 1877 and 1878. Few people knew him at all, and of those who did, few found anything particularly likeable about him. Some theorized that he had come to the Panhandle to escape the revenge of an enemy. Others whispered of a tragedy in his past, a woman from the East who had died or left him.

152

Springer's Ranch was located on the old military trail between Ft. Elliott and Ft. Supply, and as the buffalo hunters moved on to better hunting grounds to the south, Springer began catering to the trade that passed up and down the trail. The place became a stop on the stage coach line, and a small post office was added in 1878 under the name of Boggy Creek Station. Springer hired a young Texan named Tom Leadbetter to help him with his various enterprises, and Springer's Ranch did a brisk business—not all of it respectable. As military traffic between the forts increased, Springer introduced whiskey and gambling to draw in the soldier trade, and before long Springer's Ranch became known as a hangout for soldiers of the Tenth Cavalry from Ft. Elliott. These black troopers flocked to Springer's establishment to escape the snubs and racial slurs of white officers and hunters around the fort. Springer welcomed their whiskey and card business and went out of his way to make them feel at home.

Springer himself was a noted card player, one who gambled hard and usually won, and although he tried to keep out of the games, he couldn't resist sitting in on a hand every now and then. He won more than he lost, and inevitably the losers went away embittered and grumbling. Maybe he was lucky, or maybe the games were actually rigged; in any case, Springer left himself open to the charge of running a crooked establishment.

There are several versions of what happened one night in the fall of 1878, and that Friday morning Mr. Conatser related the one his father told him years ago.

"This party of colored soldiers came by Springer's place and asked if they could camp close by. Springer said sure, he was glad to have them. That night they got into a big card game and Springer won all their money. They thought he had cheated them, but they left without saying anything. The next morning they talked it over and decided to go back for their money. They got into an argument and Springer came out shooting. The soldiers returned the fire, and when the smoke cleared Springer and Leadbetter went down. The soldiers left them and rode away. The bodies were found by a stagecoach driver. At the next stop down the line, he got two men named Robinson and Fry to go back and bury them. When they got there, they found spur tracks in the dirt where Leadbetter had crawled around the room before he died."

On November 30, 1878, the *Dodge City Times* reported,

The inquest which was composed of respectable citizens of the neighborhood, have rendered their verdict that Springer fired the first two shots, and that Mr. Leadbetter the other victim, was in the act of preventing Springer from shooting at the soldiers when he received his wound. The inquest board have entirely exonerated the soldiers from any blame whatever, as they acted purely in self-defense.

Today nothing remains of Springer's Ranch but the story, a few square nails and cartridge jackets, and a granite marker over the graves of Springer and Leadbetter—in the front yard of Tom Conatser's ranch house.[1]

XX

Oasis Ranch and Needmore Creek

After a big lunch of roast beef, roasting ears, potatoes, biscuits and molasses, we all hunted a cool spot and bagged a few hours of sleep. Then, around five that afternoon, Bill and I loaded our horses and rode east toward the Oasis Ranch on the Oklahoma line. Getting into the saddle that day proved something less than a pleasure, as my rump, thighs, and shoulders ached from their encounter with the bucking barrel.

From the heavily wooded bottoms of Boggy Creek, we rode into a rolling hill country with red soil and tall luxurious grasses. Around six-thirty we looked off to the south and saw the freshly painted red guest houses at the headquarters of the Big Bull Ranch. Established in 1893 by Tom Conatser's father and J. H. Hopkins, the Big Bull was acquired by Gene "Old Tack" Howe during the Depression. Howe, an avid sportsman, constructed dams and lakes, built the guest houses, and made it into something of a hunting resort. Among the guests he entertained at the Big Bull were Robert Taylor and Clark Gable.

Around sundown we topped a hill and enjoyed a full view of what some people call the most beautiful ranch in the Panhandle. The Oasis Ranch lay on both sides of Oasis Creek, and the headquarters was located in a green valley overlooking a spring-fed lake. The creek was named by Colonel Nelson Miles during the Indian wars of 1874. In a letter dated August 25, 1874, Colonel Miles wrote,

Bill Ellzey's footprints are the only marks on this large sand dune in a sandy stretch of country north of the river between Boggy Creek and the Oasis Ranch.

With a possibility of this campaign lasting during Autumn and Winter, I would suggest the propriety of establishing a supply camp on a beautiful creek, which I have denominated Oasis Creek, about ten miles west of Antelope Hills, on the north side of the Canadian, where any desired amount of hay can be cured, and supplies stored.

There is abundance of timber, fine water and grazing, and the point is accessible and central for military operations in this vicinity.[1]

We arrived at the Oasis headquarters and found Hunky Green just as he was going out to do his evening chores. A handsome man whose prematurely graying hair added a touch of distinction to his youthful face, Hunky operated the ranch for the owner, Bill McQuiddy of Perryton. As we were putting up the horses for the night, I asked Hunky about his unusual name. He gave this explanation: he, was born Henry Green; Henry was shortened to Hank, Hank shortened to Hunk, and Hunk sweetened to Hunky. And that is how the world got its first Hunky Green.

When we had taken care of the horses, Hunky fetched a gallon bucket full of milk and headed down to a stall in the barn. There he showed us a Red Brangus bull calf about two weeks old, and hung the bucket on a nail on the wall. While the calf went to work hungrily on the mechanical teat at the bottom of the bucket, Hunky told us what had happened to the calf's mother.

About two weeks before, Hunky had ridden out to check some heifers that were heavy with their first calves. Occasionally a first-calf heifer will have difficulty delivering her calf, and the cowboy has to watch them closely. That day Hunky found a heifer stretched out on the ground, just a few heartbeats away from death. By the time he had gotten down from his horse and looked the situation over, she had expired. This was a good heifer and he knew the calf would be a good one, so he decided to perform a cesarean, on the slim chance that he might be able to save the calf. He whipped out his pocket knife, rolled up his sleeves, and cut into the dead heifer. He rescued the calf, dried him off, and carried him back to the house. Two weeks later, we found the calf strong and healthy, and his surrogate mother beaming with pride.

It was dusk by the time we got up to the house, and we found that Ann, Hunky's wife, had prepared supper for us.

After the meal, we played a few games of chess and talked about the river.

The next morning, after wolfing down several pans of Ann's luscious sourdough biscuits, we went for a drive over the ranch, and Hunky told us a yarn he'd heard a few years back. During the Dust Bowl days there was a fellow named Roy working on an outfit along the river. One day while he and another man were out looking for strays, they rode up to a little cow camp. Roy hadn't eaten all day and was about to starve, and when he saw a big beautiful ham hanging on the front porch, his eyes bugged out and his mouth began to water. After a few minutes' thought, he convinced himself that the camp was abandoned and the ham would go to waste unless he "saved" it. So he cut the rope and rode away with the ham under his arm.

Later that day a dust storm moved in from the north, one of the biggest and blackest storms the country had ever seen. When it hit, the sun was swallowed up and the day turned to night. In the gloom, Roy and his companion stumbled into a buffalo wallow and took cover. Roy was shaking all over. "Well, this is it," he moaned. "This is bound to be the end of the world."

The other man swallowed hard and nodded. "I guess it is."

Roy looked down at the ham and began to regret that he had "saved" it on the last day of the world. Not only would he not have a chance to eat it, but when the Roll was called up Yonder, the Lord just might think he had *stolen* it. Roy didn't need any more sins on his record. "Say, listen," he turned to his friend, "maybe we ought to say some prayers or something. You know how to pray?"

He shook his head. "Naw, Roy, I never done much of it myself. How about you, can you pray?"

"Well, I used to could."

"Then you better do it. You pray for both of us."

Roy pressed his lips together. "Well, all right," he replied. "You hold the ham and I'll pray."

✿   ✿   ✿

On Sunday morning we loaded up the horses and bid farewell to the Oasis Ranch. From Plemons we had followed the river valley all the way to the Oklahoma state line, and now it was time to turn back west and ride to our final destination, the town of Canadian. Hunky saddled up his big buckskin horse and rode with us down to the river. Along the way we jumped a coyote and Hunky gave chase in hopes of roping it, but the old coyote ducked under a fence and put an end to the race.

From Oasis Creek we followed the riverbed fifteen miles west. At first I was glad we would have the chance to spend so much time in the bottom, since up until that time we had only crossed it a couple of times. But as the day progressed, my thinking began to change. As usual we had spent too much time talking that morning and hadn't gotten away until ten o'clock, which threw our travel time in the hottest part of the day. And we soon discovered that the riverbed was a bad place to be in the heat of the day. We found the bottom humid and utterly without a cooling breeze. The combination of sand and heavy brush made the trip hard on the horses, and of course we had deer flies to contend with every step of the way.

American folklore abounds in songs and stories about lazy rivers and mighty rivers and quiet rivers and rivers that call you back to the pleasant memories of childhood. The Canadian has inspired nothing like this. It is a wicked, perverse, stingy river. Stephen Foster couldn't have written a sweet little ditty about the Canadian; he would have been too busy swatting at deer flies. If Mark Twain had sent Huck and Jim down the Canadian, American literature would have been deprived of its best example of River-As-Universal-Being; Huck and Jim would not have found enough water to float a feather, much less a raft.

Around four o'clock we rode out of the bottom and followed Needmore Creek two miles south to the John Isaacs ranch. John Isaacs was an amiable man with a crew cut and a pair of elfish blue-gray eyes. He saw us coming up the road and met us at the corral. When we had put up the horses, he took us out in the pasture and called up his old longhorn steer, Roany, which he kept around as a pet. A direct descendant of that hardy breed of cattle that could transport themselves to market and still put on flesh, Roany looked odd and out of place standing next to the shorter, stockier beef animals of the 1970s. But in their era, these long-legged, big-boned creatures fed the nation, walking distances that would have killed their higher-blooded British cousins.

The Isaacses lived in a modern one-story house on a hill above Needmore Creek. Like many dwellings along the river, it was originally a two- or three-room house, built by parents and grandparents, with extra rooms added over the years when the grass and price of cattle permitted. One of the rooms in the old part of the house was paneled with boxcar siding. Over the hearth hung a six-foot span of longhorns. John Isaacs finished and mounted them himself, buying the raw horns from a man down-state. He mounted horns as a hobby and had sold a few sets and given others to friends for Christmas. But he had managed to keep five or six pair for himself, and they hung in all parts of the house, along with a set of buffalo horns given to him by a descendant of a local buffalo hunter.

John Isaacs had an uncle named George who figured prominently in one of the most famous stories ever to come out of Hemphill County. I had been told that the Isaacs family wouldn't discuss the Canadian Depot Robbery with outsiders, but after supper, when we had pushed our chairs back from the table and made ourselves comfortable, I decided to ask about it anyway. And what do you know. He told us the whole story.

XXI

The Canadian Depot Robbery

George Isaacs had three brothers who settled in Hemphill County and became landowners and respected citizens. But somehow things had never worked out right for George. At the time his brothers had been settling on land, he had been over in Randall County cowboying for the T Anchor Ranch. That had been a good life, an exciting life, and he had worked his way up to a responsible position on the T Anchor. But when the time came for him to think about marrying and settling down, he discovered that all the good land in the Panhandle had already been bought up. He envied the prosperity and solid respectability of his brothers and told himself that they had just been lucky. Good judgement and hard work might have come closer to explaining their success, but George couldn't bring himself to admit that, since it would have carried with it an implicit criticism of himself. George had never been blessed with good judgement, but instead of admitting it, he went on compounding mistakes with more mistakes and explaining the world in terms of good and bad luck.

By the year 1896 when the story opens, he had taken a wife, sired several children, and acquired a little hardscrabble farm in Indian Territory. He was tired of farming and pressed for money. As usual, he found an explanation outside himself; the country was sorry, the drought had bitten him, the grasshoppers had singled his crops out for destruction, he'd just

The John Isaacs family in their ranch home in Needmore Creek east of Canadian. Mr. Isaacs' uncle George Isaacs was involved in one of the most famous stories ever to come out of Hemphill County: the Canadian Depot Robbery.

suffered a run of bad luck, that was all. With a little time and some quick cash, he could get ahead of the game.

Before Indian Territory became the state of Oklahoma, it was a refuge for outlaws, from cattle rustlers and horse thieves to train robbers and bank robbers. It drew a restless breed of men who could appreciate George Isaacs' quick-cash-and-get-ahead view of the world. George himself was not an outlaw, and left to himself he might never have gotten into serious trouble. But stripped of the niceties of rhetoric, his philosophy of life and that of the outlaws differed only slightly, and that was primarily in the fact that George confined himself to carping about his bad luck, while the outlaws were more inclined to do something about theirs.

So, perhaps it was inevitable that the two finally found each other. One night two men named Jim Stanley and Bill Doolen appeared on the front porch of the Isaacs house and said they had something to talk over with George. We might imagine that George was hesitant at first. He didn't know these men and he didn't particularly like their looks. But he was the kind of man who was always looking for auguries that would signal the beginning of his good fortune, and he simply couldn't deny fate the chance of finding him.

Stanley and Doolen outlined their plan. Suppose a man shipped some cattle to Kansas City and sold them for, say, $500. Now, if a man was careful, he wouldn't carry that kind of money on his return trip; he'd deposit it at the express company office and let them transport it home in a guarded express car. And if the train happened to be robbed, he could always get his money out of the express company. That was the normal way of doing business. Smart cattlemen did it all the time. But just suppose a man had told the express company that he was shipping $25,000 instead of $500; if the train were robbed, he would get $25,000 back. Now, that was a quick and easy way of making money without hurting anyone but the express company, and they were big enough to absorb the loss.

George must have thought this was the perfect crime. His part was easy. All he had to do was deposit the money with the express company and collect on the loss. Stanley and Doolen would rob the train, and they assured him there would be no bloodshed. There was no way it couldn't work.

In subsequent meetings the details of the crime were firmed up. Around the twentieth of November, George would ship a

163

small number of cattle to the Kansas City market, enough to bring about $500. The money would be sent by express to Canadian and George would ride the same train. Canadian was chosen for several reasons. A small town, it had only one sheriff; it was far enough away from their home base in Indian Territory to confuse the authorities; yet it was close enough to the state line so that the robbers could escape Texas law. Furthermore, George had family living there, which not only gave him a convenient excuse for going there, but also a place to hide in case something went wrong.

In Kansas City, George sold the cattle to a commission company, cashed the check for $500, and checked into a hotel for the night. After locking the door behind him and pulling down the shades, he laid out five stacks of paper strips, the size of a currency bill, and on top of each stack he placed a few ten-dollar bills. Then he put each stack in a box, wrapped and sealed it, and marked "$5,000" on the outside of each. The next morning he deposited the "$25,000" at the express company office. The teller did not count the money because he recognized the name Isaacs. Apparently he had done business with George's brothers and knew that they were reputable cattlemen.

George and the money rode the same train to Canadian, and when it stopped at the station he hurried away and checked in at a hotel in town. We might imagine that as he signed his name in the guest register, he heard gunshots echoing up the street.

Jim Stanley had ridden into town that evening with three men: Jim Harbolt, Bill Doolen, and Tulsey Jack Blake. A woman had seen them down by the stockyards and had reported it to Sheriff Tom McGee, who had already been notified that a large shipment of cash was coming in on the train. Concerned about the report of strangers lurking down by the stockyards, he went to the station to investigate. What happened then is not clear, but Sheriff McGee was shot dead and the robbery was aborted. The robbers made a run for their horses and galloped out of town. Late that night Hugh Burton, a horse wrangler for the Laurel Leaf Ranch, was awakened by four men. They said they were going to trade their jaded horses for four fresh ones from the remuda. Burton saw that they were armed and did not try to stop them. The men saddled the fresh horses and rode on east to the state line.

The next day the whole town of Canadian was buzzing with the story of Tom McGee's murder. At nine o'clock in the

164

morning the commissioners' court held a special meeting to examine the contents of the packages that had come in with the express shipment. When they discovered the phoney paper inside, they ordered the arrest of George Isaacs on a charge of murder. The trial was held in Hardeman County in the district court of Judge J. M. Standlee. Under an indictment for murder, George Isaacs was charged with one count as principal and one count as accomplice. The jury found him guilty. Attorneys for the defense filed some fifty bills of exception and assignments of error in the record, and the case was taken to the Texas Court of Criminal Appeals. After studying the record and the bills of exception, Justice Hurt upheld the conviction. George Isaacs went to the state penitentiary to serve a life sentence.[1]

But George wasn't finished yet. After serving two weeks of his life sentence, he was freed on a pardon signed in the governor's hand—only the governor hadn't signed it. The document was a forgery. It wasn't discovered until a month later, and although the governor was furious and demanded that the prisoner be brought to justice, by that time George had fled to Arizona Territory.

Who forged the pardon? Almost a year to the day after John Isaacs told us this story, I received a letter from a man named Clyde Hodges, a farmer in Roberts County who had heard of my interest in the Canadian Depot Robbery. "I can tell you the man's name who went to the prison and forged the governor's name and got George Isaacs out of the pen," he wrote. "It was my dad's cousin Billy Washington. I have heard my dad, the late George Hodges, tell about what Billy told him many times." A few days later I drove out to the Hodges place west of Miami and listened to the story of Billy Washington.

On July 31, 1949, the *Daily Oklahoman* ran an article on an old house in Marietta, Oklahoma, which it called one of the most unusual homes in the state. The house was built in 1888 by William E. Washington, "one of the fabulous cattle kings of pre-statehood days in the Chickasaw Indian nation." Washington, the article said, "was a combination of the often ruthless, sometimes softhearted men of an era when you got all the grassland you could take and hold." He was married to a full-blooded Chickasaw Indian woman and started his empire on Indian lands. Controlling a huge spread, he employed as many as a hundred cowboys and laborers and paid them in his own paper

165

and pewter currency, which was negotiable in stores and commissaries on the ranch. In 1886 Washington began construction of the house in Marietta, which took two years to build and cost $50,000, an enormous sum of money for the times. It contained beautifully inlaid hardwood floors, speaking tubes in every room, and walls filled with gravel to a height of six feet.

The gravel in the walls was not insulation, but to prevent someone from shooting into the house. Billy Washington had acquired a fortune in land and cattle, and in the process had made a number of enemies. It was said that he killed several men in his lifetime, one of whom he shot in the throat at the railroad depot in El Reno, Oklahoma. Until the day he died, Billy carried a .45 pistol in a cloth scabbard sewed on the inside of his pants. Such a man could never enjoy a quiet evening in a house with thin walls.

I don't know exactly how or why Billy Washington became involved in the misfortunes of George Isaacs. It is possible that he knew George in Indian Territory and was involved in the Canadian Depot Robbery from the very beginning, and that he forged Isaacs' pardon to get him out of the country before he revealed too much. This would make a fine story, but unfortunately there is no proof that it happened this way. It is more likely that by 1896 he had lost his fortune and was in need of money. One way or another he arranged with the Isaacs family to forge the pardon for a price.

Billy Washington was a millionaire at the age of thirty-eight, and he made and lost a fortune three times during his life. From Oklahoma he moved to Carlsbad, New Mexico, where he established another large ranch and built another palatial mansion. But there his fortunes declined again. Enemies burned down his house and he lost all but his two-hundred-acre homestead. In the late 1940s he died in poverty, leaving his Indian wife to live in a mud house amid the desolation of the New Mexico desert. Shortly after Billy's death, the roof of the house caved in and buried her.

And what about George Isaacs? One day many years after the Canadian Depot Robbery, George's son happened to be in San Antonio. As he walked down the street, he met a ruined old man, his father, who had never returned to his family in Oklahoma. He gave the old man a twenty-dollar bill and went on. Here the books close on George Isaacs, as he was never seen or heard from again.

XXII

Canadian

Queen City of the Panhandle

We arose the next morning at six, ate a good hearty breakfast, and began the last leg of our journey, a ten-mile ride into Canadian. A thunderstorm the night before had left the country cool and damp, the sky a gray overcast. The horses felt frisky in the morning air and we made good time, arriving in Canadian around ten-thirty or eleven.

Compared to the towns of New England or Virginia, Canadian was hardly more than a child. While Bostonians were reading Emerson by gas light, Uncle Dick Bussell was hunting buffalo on what is now Canadian's courthouse square. In 1888, the year the world saw its first copy of *National Geographic*, Canadian was nothing more than a sprawl of tents and shacks along the Santa Fe Railroad. But in 1972, at the age of eighty-five, it was one of the oldest towns in the northern Panhandle; also one of its most picturesque and interesting. It had character, grace, and elegance, and the mellow flavor that age brings to a place. You could see it in the old Victorian houses, in the red brick streets, in the people, and in the stories that took root in the tracks of the last buffalo herds.

Drew Cantwell was one of the characters who gave Canadian its unique flavor. At the age of sixteen he went to work as a blacksmith, making his living over a coal forge. Out of

On the Oasis Ranch, Erickson and Ellzey stand with one foot in Oklahoma and one in Texas beside a cement boundary marker. The Oklahoma state line was the easternmost point on their fifteen-day, 140-mile horseback ride down the Canadian River.

pitchforks, rake teeth, and Model T springs, he made spurs and bridle bits which he sold to local cowboys. For thirty years he was a mechanic at Hobdy Motor Company and moonlighted as the village fix-it man. By the time he retired, he had established a reputation as a man who could fix anything.

Consider this example. In the early 1950s an employee at a bank in Canadian made a grave mistake: he disconnected the time lock on the bank's currency safe. This burglar-proof safe, about the size of a wash tub, contained all the bank's notes, securities, and money. Borrowing enough cash to conduct business, the frantic bank president called the factory for help. The factory representative came and delivered some sad news. The safe, constructed of manganese steel 2½ inches thick, could be entered with an acetylene torch, but the heat necessary to melt a hole in the steel would destroy the papers inside. That is why the safe was called burglar-proof. As a last resort, the bank president called in Drew Cantwell, who had never opened a safe in his life, but who had an uncanny gift for fixing the unfixable.

Working all night with his torch, Cantwell cut and cooled the metal until he had a hole in the top of the safe. He made a key out of welding rod, inserted it into the hole, and unlocked the time lock case. Then he fashioned a hook out of welding rod and sprung the latch holding the door. The safe was opened, and not one paper or bill inside was burned or even scorched. His secret: to concentrate the heat in a small area, he made a paste of asbestos powder and water and applied it around the edges of the hole.

For opening the safe that couldn't be opened, for putting the bank back in business, he was paid $80.

In the spring of 1972, when Mr. Cantwell was 67, he took me on a tour of the three shops where he did all his repair work. He told me, with considerable pride, that he had never advertised his repair business, had never wanted for work, and had never hired any outside help. As we went through his shops, I jotted down a list of articles I saw. It will give the reader an idea of the number and variety of contraptions he was working on at this particular time:

    21 clocks
    7 Edison phonographs
    4 player pianos

2 jukeboxes
8 record players
1 television set
2 adding machines
6 electric fans
1 typewriter
1 hot plate
4 organs
1 vacuum sweeper
2 radios
1 piano
1 milk shake mixer
1 cash register
3 air conditioners
1 fruit scale

While I was there, a man called to ask if Cantwell would repair his John Deere tractor, another dropped in to pick up his water pump, and a lady came by and left clock number 22.

His philosophy in this business was refreshing and unique. If something was broken, it could be fixed; if he didn't have a service manual, he would use his own wits to figure out how the device worked; if he couldn't buy parts, he would make them himself. I asked him if he had ever been brought an item which he had not been able to fix. He scratched his chin and said, "Yes, a pair of false teeth."

Around 1964 a man brought in an old player piano and asked Cantwell to restore it for him. Cantwell knew nothing about player pianos, but he studied it and tinkered with it and rebuilt it from the ground up. By 1972, when I met him, he had restored over a hundred player pianos and player organs, and had become one of perhaps a dozen men in the United States who specialized in restoring these antique instruments.

The player piano is a complex instrument which uses vacuum as a power source. Instructions cut on paper rolls are fed into a kind of computer which routes vacuum through a network of tubes, activating beaters which strike the strings. Made in the early part of this century, the player piano was able to create music without transistors, wires, or electricity—and also without a musician.

Most people associate the player piano with rinky-tink saloon music, but the same vacuum which reproduces saloon music can also be applied to classical works. Several years back, Cantwell bought an Aeolian-Webber reproducing grand piano, a piece of junk when he found it. He stripped it down to a shell and rebuilt it in his living room. This instrument reproduced a piece of music just as it was played by a virtuoso musician. With its vacuum "brain" and four accordion bellows, it made five separate operations simultaneously, recreating not only the notes, but also the contrast and expression of the artist.

But Drew Cantwell was not satisfied with restoring and rebuilding player instruments. Around 1970 he saw a picture of a rare device called a Coinola which applied the player piano principle to more than one instrument. He couldn't rest until he had made one for himself. Starting with an old player piano, he spent a year building mountings, beaters, bellows, and installing over seven hundred feet of tubing. When he had finished, he had a player *orchestra* composed of eleven small instruments: piano, bass drum, cymbals, snare drum, wood block, castanets, tambourine, triangle, mandolin rail, and xylophone. The entire orchestra was self-contained inside a plexiglass case which he built on top of the piano. As a convenience, Cantwell hooked up the bellows mechanism to an electric motor so that, at the flick of a switch, he could sit down and enjoy the rollicking music of a bygone era, with eleven instruments playing as if by magic.

Building a self-playing orchestra was not a bad trick for a man who had a seventh grade education, could not read a note of music, or play a musical instrument. I was highly impressed.

"Mr. Cantwell," I said, "somebody ought to write a story about you. This is unbelievable!"

I shall never forget his response. He looked at me very seriously and replied, "Oh tut."

✿   ✿   ✿

Bill and I stabled the horses at a little place Drew Cantwell owned on the east edge of town and started walking down Cheyenne Street. At Main we turned north and headed for the downtown area. We passed the old Studer mansion, a big brooding three-story house that stood on top of a hill, staring across the street at the windowless weed-choked Mary B. Isaacs school. They sat there like an old couple in the twilight of life, sharing their memories of another century as teenagers zoomed

171

past in Chargers and Mustangs. In the next block we passed Frank McMordie's elegant old red brick house with its tile roof; on past the Women's Christian Temperance Union Hall; and then on to the courthouse square. Beyond the square, the business district began and Main Street followed a steep hill that ended three blocks below at the Santa Fe Depot. We continued down the hill and passed the pool hall where I had first met Charlie Tubb.

When I met him in 1971, Charlie was ninety-four years old. Born in England in 1877, he came to this country on a sailboat at the age of four. His family moved to Hemphill County and spent several nights at Springer's Ranch (Springer had been dead for several years, but his place was still being used as a stage stop). One of the oldest of the old-timers, Charlie Tubb took devilish delight in doing things that a nice old man was not supposed to do. In Canadian, a bastion of Protestantism, he once stood at the door of the post office, passing out atheist literature to everyone who came by. This created a scandal and earned him the reputation of being an irreverent man, and he was just ornery enough to enjoy every minute of it. A retired rancher and businessman, he spent a lot of time at the pool hall, and the day I met him he challenged me to a game of snooker and gave me a romping I won't soon forget. Nibbling at a quid of plug tobacco, his eyes crackling with glee, he ran the last four balls and chalked his winning score on the blackboard. I got the impression he rather enjoyed putting the young whippersnappers in their place. For me it was a unique experience; I had never been beaten at snooker by a man ninety-four years old, who was old enough to have known Charles Goodnight— and had.

In 1967, at the age of ninety, Charlie Tubb decided he wanted to see some of the world. Traveling alone, he drove to San Francisco, flew to Sydney, Australia, and spent fifty-seven days looking over the country Down Under. One of the things that impressed him most about Australia was that the whole time he was there, he didn't hear a single swear word. "All they ever say over there is 'bloody bloke,'" he observed.

Upon his return to Canadian, he added another chapter to the Tubb legend by writing a delightfully outrageous letter to the local newspaper. In this letter he offered to bet anyone in town a thousand dollars that he would live to be a hundred years old. "Anyone wishing to take this bet must buy E. Government Bonds and deposit them in the First State Bank, Canadian, Texas, in Escrow," he wrote. "It is understood that . . . the demise must be of natural nature."[1] No one took him up on the bet. One woman expressed interest but backed out when she learned of the natural causes part of the agreement. "I think she planned to run over me," he told me, grinning wickedly. Charlie would have lost the bet. He died in 1973 at the age of ninety-six.

Charlie Tubb was one of a kind. I once asked him to what he attributed his long life. "I didn't have a damn thing to do with it," he snorted. "On my mother's side I come from a good breed of dogs, that's all."

❉   ❉   ❉

Bill and I crossed Main Street and walked into the office of the *Canadian Record* where we were warmly received by Ben and Nancy Ezzell, the charming couple who had operated the *Record* for the past twenty-five years. I had first heard of Ben Ezzell back in the late Fifties and had always thought of him as a kind of Hodding Carter in the Texas Panhandle, a stubborn, courageous, independent journalist who applied the highest standards of his craft to a small-town weekly.

The Ezzells had promised us a bed, a bath, and a beer when we ended our trip, and we had come to collect on the promise—in reverse order. That evening in the Ezzell living room, we raised our flagons and toasted the expedition, and enjoyed the blessing of good friends and companionship.

The next morning was the Fourth of July, the biggest day of the year in the town of Canadian. Around ten we drove down to the *Record* office, and while Bill and Ben Ezzell discussed cameras and darkrooms, I slipped outside to have a look around. Outside, a crisp north wind and a cover of low gray clouds promised to take the sweat out of this Fourth of July celebration and threatened to end it altogether. It had rained about an inch in the night, and the clouds appeared capable of dropping another inch or two before the day was over.

Main Street was practically deserted in this hour before the parade began. Mud-spattered pickups pulling stock trailers passed down the hill, and cars carrying brightly decorated bicycles and wide-eyed children headed toward the gathering point of the parade. Down the street at the old Moody Hotel, country music blared through crackly loud speakers, as people dropped in to register for the Old Settlers' Reunion. American flags were out on every corner and rodeo banners flapped lazily over the pool hall, the Palace Barber Shop, the bank, the Miracle Beauty "Salone," and the *Record* office.

I hiked up the hill to the courthouse to get a better view of the town. From this vantage point I could see a lot of things, and most of them were made of dark red brick. Main Street was paved with red brick and most of the buildings I could see were made from it: the courthouse, the jail, the WCTU Hall, the First Christian Church, and many of the houses around the square. The town fathers must have gotten a discount at the red brick factory.

The walk around the square reminded me of stories I had heard about this town. Take the WCTU Hall across the street, the only structure in the nation which was built, owned, and still operated by a local chapter of the Women's Christian Temperance Union (which was still meeting every fourth Wednesday of the month). Ben McIntyre tells the story about a social the WCTU ladies gave years ago, when some elf primed a big bowl of punch with grain alcohol. That is one of Ben's better yarns.

And then there was the tale about the town's first temperance election in 1903. Up until the election day Canadian had been a wide open little town, with saloons, gambling halls, and houses of ill repute. Feelings ran high on both sides, as the Drys campaigned to clean up the town. The Wets were just as determined to keep it dirty. The night of the election, a large crowd of men gathered on Main Street to follow the counting of the ballots and hear the results. When it was announced that the town had voted itself dry, the crowd suddenly became an angry mob. The men went home for their guns, and for several hours Canadian hovered between war and peace. But finally the sheriff persuaded them to go home and that ended that. To this day, Canadian remains theoretically dry.

On the south side of the square, at the intersection of Fourth and Main, Jim Derrick and Sheriff Case met one day long ago to settle their differences with blazing six-shooters. As the shots rang out, pedestrians dived behind trees and into ditches to dodge the flying lead—all but Mrs. Groom, a very proper English lady who wore her hair piled high on her head. She either wasn't aware of the brawl or figured that if the two men were gentlemen they would stop trying to kill each other and allow her to cross the street. When she reached the middle of the street, a stray bullet struck her down. Horrified, Case and Derrick forgot their differences and rushed to her side, only to discover that the bullet had punctured her hairdo and nothing more.

And the big red brick courthouse reminded me of a celebrated case which was tried inside: City of Canadian v. Harrison Guthrie, or as it is known in these parts, The Case of Guthrie's One-Eyed Mare.

Guthrie was a poor man who hauled wood for a living. His assets in this business included a rickety old wagon and a one-eyed mare, age twelve or fourteen years. In 1930 the citizens of Canadian began to complain that Guthrie's mare was leaving her pen at night and grazing on lawns, shrubbery, and flowers. When these complaints reached city hall, the mare was arrested and placed in the city pound. When Guthrie failed to come forward with the pound fee, the city hired a man named Panhandle Pete Lemley to take the mare outside of town and shoot her, which he did. The case might have ended there, with a poor man deprived of his only means of making a living, had it not attracted the attention of a local attorney named E. J. Cussen, another of those remarkable characters who somehow ended up in the little town of Canadian.

Cussen was first called to my attention by Mike Harter, a kinsman of mine and a scholar of Texas Catholicism, who ran across some canon law documents relating to Cussen in the Texas Catholic Archives in Austin. It seems that around 1910 Cussen was ordained as a priest and took his first assignment in Abilene in West Texas, where he developed a drinking problem. On a visit to the University of Dallas he staggered into the priests' refectory and was reprimanded by his superiors. Later he was arrested in Fort Worth and the chancellor of the diocese had to bail him out of jail.

At this point Bishop Lynch of Dallas decided that Father Cussen needed to be removed from civilization, and so he arranged in 1918 to have him transferred to Canadian. Here Cussen took his first parish, but even in this new setting he did not mend his ways, and word of further scandal reached the chancery in Dallas. Bishop Lynch dashed off a canon law precept which, in essence, told the renegade priest to straighten up or face grave consequences. Father Cussen did not straighten up, so the bishop suspended him, ordered him out of Canadian, and commanded him to retire at once to the Trappist Monastery at Gethsemane, Kentucky. Cussen not only refused to leave but challenged the bishop's power to remove him, provoking a canon law case which ended up at the Apostolic Delegate in Washington, D.C. Cussen's plea was rejected, but still he refused to leave his Canadian mission, and Bishop Lynch dispatched two Irish priests, the O'Brien brothers, to move in and retake the mission. It is said that Father Cussen chased Father Tom O'Brien off the premises with a pitchfork.

Eventually Cussen was removed from the bishop's property, but he did not leave Canadian, much to the displeasure of the local Catholics. Instead, he married a good Presbyterian woman, gave up alcohol, and eventually joined the law firm of Hoover and Hoover. He lived and practiced law in Canadian until his death in 1958.

I don't know why Cussen decided to make his home on the Canadian River in the Texas Panhandle, but it had nothing to do with lack of choice. Educated at the University of London and Oxford, he took a doctorate at the Sorbonne and possessed a brilliant classical education. According to his obituary, he fought in the Spanish-American War and the Boer War and served in the French Foreign Legion. With this kind of background, he probably could have practiced law in any major city in the United States, yet something about the little town on the Canadian River captured his imagination, and it was here that he chose to live out his life.

And why did this man, who had studied in the finest universities in Europe, take on the case of Guthrie's One-Eyed Mare? Ben Ezzell and Bill Jackson, both of whom knew Cussen well, believed that he saw the case as a kind of toy which gave him an opportunity to play his own erudition off against the legal system at its lowest level, while at the same time giving his poor client a well-argued defense. While the attorney for the City of Canadian argued his case in earnest legal prose, the record shows Mr. Cussen addressing the court in *verse*: filing a motion for a rehearing of the case, Cussen wrote,

Comes now the plaintiff, appellee,
And moves this Honorable Court to see,
That House Bill Number 304
Threw open wide the Court House door,
Of County Court in Hemphill County

Where Guthrie sought relief and bounty,
And recompense and generous meed,
For his departed wayward steed,
Cut down in all her youthful pride,
When she was taken for a ride.

The court did hold, that as this mare,
To wrong curtilage did repair,
Likewise, these lawyers who here do pray,
In the wrong court below did stray;
But this Honorable Court overlooked the fact,
That the Legislature passed an Act,
In Nineteen Hundred and Fifteen,
And Jurisdiction since has been,
In that Court whence this case came,
As in the Justice Court the same.

Cussen took the case to the Court of Civil Appeals in Amarillo. The City of Canadian was forced to pay sixty-five dollars to Harrison Guthrie.[2]

* * *

By this time it was almost eleven o'clock and I walked on down to Second Street to watch the parade with Bill Ellzey and Ben Ezzell, whom I found roosting on the fire escape of the Moody Hotel and snapping pictures of the crowd. Before the parade began, I ran into Woods King on the corner and asked how he was enjoying the celebration. It was fine, he said, and then told me of the first time he could remember coming to Canadian—in 1893.

A few minutes after eleven the parade began, led by five war veterans from the local post carrying the colors. Next came all the city and county fire trucks blowing their sirens and clanging their bells; then the bicycles and tricycles, go-carts, wagons, and riding lawn mowers; floats and antique cars, followed by a legion of horses and riders: the local roping club, the rodeo queen, local cowboys and cowgirls, the Lipscomb County Riding Club, the Llano Estacado Arabian Horse Club, women riding side saddle, and then every kid in town who had managed to beg or borrow a horse for the big occasion. At the rear of the horse contingent, in the position of honor, came the celebrity of the day, a weather forecaster from a television station in Amarillo. As he passed, he drew a rustle of applause

177

from the crowd and this wry comment from Woods King: "Well, he's a lot like me. Hell of a good old boy, but he don't know much about the weather."

At two o'clock that afternoon I was in the rodeo stands braving the cold—yes, on the Fourth of July, I was wrapped in a blanket—while Bill roamed the arena with his camera. Canadian is no stranger to rodeo, and in fact the claim has been made that the first rodeo in Texas was held in Canadian in the summer of 1888, when cowboys from the Laurel Leaf Ranch held a public contest at the Santa Fe stockyards. Rodeo scholars might dispute this claim (see *Persimmon Hill* magazine, volume 5, number 2, page 86), but rodeo has been a part of Canadian since the very beginning. In 1922 J. C. Studer established his Anvil Park Rodeo, a professional show on the RCA circuit for more than twenty years. After World War II Anvil Park shut down and the rodeo moved to the arena east of town, where it has become a community-sponsored affair open to amateur cowboys and cowgirls.

At four o'clock the rodeo came to an end. The ropers and riders loaded up their rigging and moved on down the highway to another rodeo in Crescent, Oklahoma, leaving behind a quiet arena and a lot of empty Dixie cups. The show was over for another year, and for Bill Ellzey and me the river trip had come to an end.

APPENDIX

The Storytellers

Vance Apple
Bill Bartlett
Bud Brainard
Ed Brainard
H. C. Brillhart, Jr.
Drew Cantwell
Mrs. Drew Cantwell
Frank Chambers
Tom Conatser
Tark Cook
Mrs. Cap Correll
Fred Cotten
Frank Cox
Mrs. B. B. Curry
Joe Day
Clark Ellzey
Lawrence Ellzey
Mozell Eslin
R. D. Eslin
Mrs. R. D. Eslin
Ben Ezzell
Nancy Ezzell
Bob Flemming
Hunky Green
J. Evetts Haley
B. L. Hance
Bill Hardin
Mike Harter
Ben Hill
Arnold Hill
Clyde Hodges
G. H. Holt
Mrs. G. H. Holt
Harold Hudson
Mrs. H. I. Hudson
John Isaacs
W. J. Jackson
Jack Jines

Sibley Jines
Walter Killebrew
Woods King
Bill Lard
H. L. Ledrick, Jr.
Lois Cambern Marsh
Albert McGarraugh
Clifford McGarraugh
Leroy McGarraugh
Scott McGarraugh
Ben McIntyre
Dale McLain
Sam McLain
Frank McMordie
W. A. McQuiddy
Clyde Mead
Clarence Morris
Floyd Morris
Hugh Parsell
Horace Rivers
G. K. Rupprecht
Roy B. Sessions
Frank Shaller
Bob Shelton
Bert Sherman
Mrs. Nona Snyder
Coy Stevens
Jim Streeter
Roger Tandy
Fred Tarbox
Cleo Tom Terry
David Trimble
Charlie Tubb
Elrick Wilson
Spencer Whippo
J. A. Whittenburg III
Alta Wood
Charles Wright

NOTES

CHAPTER TWO
Shine Popejoy

[1]My version of the killing of Bill Parks comes from Harold Hudson, editor of the *Perryton Herald*. As a child Mr. Hudson witnessed the shooting and was kind enough to show me an unpublished manuscript he had written on the event.

[2]Information on the murder of John A. Holmes and the events that followed came from the *Borger Daily Herald*, September 15, 1929, through October 14, 1929.

[3]Records of legal action against Popejoy can be found in the district clerk's office for Hutchinson County (in Stinnett, Texas), nos. 45, 63, 326, 657, and 688.

[4]Other sources on Borger, Plemons, and Hutchinson County include: John McCarty's *Adobe Walls Bride*; Laura V. Hamner's *Light 'N Hitch*; Pauline and R. L. Robertson's *Panhandle Pilgrimage*; *Accent West* magazine, April–May, 1977; and the *Borger News-Herald*, October 15, 1972. Portions of this chapter appeared as an article in *True West* magazine, January, 1974.

CHAPTER THREE
Carson Creek

[1]My account of Kit Carson's battle on the Canadian follows Mildred Mayhall, *Indian Wars of Texas*; also Mayhall's *The Kiowas* and Stanley Vestal's *Kit Carson*. A good account of the battle appears in Robertson and Robertson's *Panhandle Pilgrimage*, an excellent and well-documented survey of Panhandle history.

CHAPTER FOUR
Billy Dixon

[1]Billy Dixon's quotations are taken from *The Life of Billy Dixon* by Olive K. Dixon.

CHAPTER FIVE
The Battle of Adobe Walls

[1]Background material on the Medicine Lodge Treaty comes from: *The Life of Billy Dixon*, pp. 41–49; *Satanta*, Clarence Wharton, pp. 81–123; *Carbine and Lance*, W. S. Nye, pp. 45–46. Material on Quanah Parker and Coyote Droppings can be found in *The Comanches*, Ernest Wallace and E. Adamson Hoebel, pp. 319–26; and *Bad Medicine and Good*, W. S. Nye, pp. 178–83.

CHAPTER SIX
Cutting for Sign

[1]Material on the Indian situation in 1860 has come primarily from Mr. Haley's *Charles Goodnight*. The story of Mrs. Sherman's death has been reported in a number of books: *Charles Goodnight*; James DeShields's *Cynthia Ann Parker*; Smythe's *Historical Sketch of Parker County*; and Wilbarger's *Indian Depredations of Texas*. In *Goodbye to a River*, John Graves gives the story a fictional touch with good results (pp. 132–39).

CHAPTER EIGHT
John's Creek Tales

[1]The story of Sena and the bear comes from John McCarty's *Adobe Walls Bride*.

[2]In *Captain Bill McDonald, Texas Ranger*, Albert Bigelow Paine discusses the Panhandle range wars on p. 158 ff.

CHAPTER ELEVEN
Government Canyon

[1]On the Panhandle Pueblo culture I have relied on Floyd V. Studer's "Discovering the Panhandle," in the annual *Panhandle-Plains Historical Review*, 1931, pp. 7–23. In *Panhandle Pilgrimage*, Mr. and Mrs. Robertson give a good account of these early Indian cultures.

CHAPTER SIXTEEN
Awanyu, Gold, and Poor George

[1]For more information on Indian cave paintings, I refer the reader to Kirkland and Newcomb's book, *The Rock Art of Texas Indians*.

[2]My account of the Santa Fe traders comes from Reuben Gold Thwaites, *Early Western Travels*, vol. 2, pp. 132–37.

CHAPTER NINETEEN
Lavender Cowboys at Springer's Ranch

[1]Other versions of the Springer story can be found in the *Panhandle-Plains Historical Review*, 1959, p. 35, and 1967, pp. 55, 56, and 87; John Cook's *The Border and the Buffalo*, pp. 94–100; Laura Hamner's *Short Grass and Longhorns*, p. 37 ff.; Angie Debo's *The Cowman's Southwest*, pp. 276–77; and Robertson and Robertson's *Panhandle Pilgrimage*, p. 198.

CHAPTER TWENTY
Oasis Ranch and Needmore Creek

[1]The quotation from Colonel Nelson Miles can be found in Joe F. Taylor's *The Indian Campaign on the Staked Plains*, pp. 19 and 20.

CHAPTER TWENTY-ONE
The Canadian Depot Robbery

[1]Justice Hurt's opinion on Isaacs v. State appears in *Southwestern Reporter*, vol. 38, pp. 40–43. (This is a law book, not a magazine, and can be found only in a legal library.) It contains a good factual account of the Canadian depot robbery.

CHAPTER TWENTY-TWO
Canadian: Queen City of the Panhandle

[1]Charlie Tubb's public wager that he would live to be a hundred appeared in the *Canadian Record*, December 21, 1967.

[2]Mike Harter's research on E. J. Cussen appears in an unpublished Master's thesis, "The Creation and Foundation of the Roman Catholic Diocese of Amarillo," pp. 56–60. Legal documents relating to Mr. Cussen's defense of Harrison Guthrie can be found in *Southwestern Reporter*, vol. 87-88, pp. 316–19; and "Brief of Appellee," no. 3839, Court of Civil Appeals for the Seventh Supreme Judicial District of Texas, Amarillo, pp. 7, 8, 33, and 34. Cussen's motion for a rehearing, written in verse, is on p. 319 of vol. 87-88 of the *Southwestern Reporter*.

BIBLIOGRAPHY

Borger Daily Herald, Borger, Texas. September 15, 1929, through October 14, 1929.

Borger News-Herald, Borger, Texas. October 15, 1972.

Canadian Record, Canadian, Texas. December 21, 1967.

Clarksville Standard, Clarksville, Texas. December 22, 1860.

Cook, John R. *The Border and the Buffalo*. Topeka: Crane and Co., 1907.

Court of Civil Appeals for the Seventh Supreme Judicial District of Texas, Amarillo. "Brief of Appellee," no. 3839, pp. 7, 8, 33, and 34.

Dallas Herald, Dallas, Texas. December 5, 1859; December 12, 1860; January 2, 1860.

Debo, Angie. *The Cowman's Southwest*. Glendale, Calif.: A. H. Clark Co., 1953.

DeShields, James. *Cynthia Ann Parker*. St. Louis: James De-Shields, 1886.

Dixon, Olive K. *The Life of Billy Dixon*. Dallas: Southwest Press, 1914. Rev. ed. 1927.

Dodge City Times. Selected news items from the Texas Panhandle, 1877–1885. Reprinted in *Panhandle-Plains Historical Review*, vol. 40 (1967), p. 55 (November 23, 1878); p. 56 (November 30, 1878); and p. 87 (April 3, 1880).

Foreman, Jim M. "The Panhandle Ghost Town." *Accent West*, April-May, 1977.

Fulton, Maurice Garland, ed. *The Diaries and Letters of Josiah Gregg*. Norman: University of Oklahoma Press, 1941.

Graves, John. *Goodbye to a River*. New York: Alfred A. Knopf, 1964.

Haley, J. Evetts. *Charles Goodnight, Cowman and Plainsman*. Boston: Houghton Mifflin, 1936.

————. *George W. Littlefield, Texan*. Norman: University of Oklahoma Press, 1943.

————. *The XIT Ranch of Texas*. Norman: University of Oklahoma Press, 1967.

Hamner, Laura V. *Light 'N Hitch*. Dallas: American Guild Press, 1958.

———. *Short Grass and Longhorns*. Norman: University of Oklahoma Press, 1943.

Harter, J. Michael. "The Creation and Foundation of the Roman Catholic Diocese of Amarillo." Master's thesis, West Texas State University, 1975.

Hudson, Harold. Unpublished manuscript on Shine Popejoy, Perryton, Texas.

Hutchinson County District Court records, Stinnett, Texas. Nos. 45, 63, 326, 657, and 688.

Kirkland, Forest, and Newcomb, William W. *The Rock Art of Texas Indians*. Austin: University of Texas Press, 1967.

McCarty, John L. *Adobe Walls Bride*. San Antonio: Naylor Co., 1955.

McMurtry, Larry. *In a Narrow Grave*. Austin: Encino Press, 1968.

Mayhall, Mildred P. *Indian Wars of Texas*. Waco: Texian Press, 1965.

———. *The Kiowas*. Norman: University of Oklahoma Press, 1962.

Miami Chief, Miami, Texas. December 3, 1970.

Nye, Wilbur Sturtevant. *Bad Medicine and Good*. Norman: University of Oklahoma Press, 1962.

———. *Carbine and Lance*. Norman: University of Oklahoma Press, 1962.

Ochiltree County Herald, Perryton, Texas. 1931–37.

Oswald, James M. "History of Ft. Elliott." *Panhandle-Plains Historical Review*, vol. 32 (1959), p. 35.

Paine, Albert Bigelow. *Captain Bill McDonald, Texas Ranger*. New York: J. J. Little and Ives Co., 1909.

Robertson, Pauline Durrett, and Robertson, R. L. *Panhandle Pilgrimage*. Canyon, Texas: Staked Plains Press, 1976.

Smythe, Henry. *Historical Sketch of Parker County*. St. Louis: L. C. Lavat, 1877.

Southwestern Reporter. Vol. 38, pp. 40–43; and vol. 87-88, pp. 316–19. St. Paul: West Publishing Co., 1914 and 1936.

Studer, Floyd. "Discovering the Panhandle." *Panhandle-Plains Historical Review*, vol. 4 (1931), pp. 7–23.

Taylor, Joe F. *The Indian Campaign on the Staked Plains, 1874–1875; Military Correspondence from War Department Adjutant General's Office, File 2815—1874.* Canyon, Texas: Panhandle-Plains Historical Society, 1962.

Thwaites, Reuben Gold. *Early Western Travels 1748–1846.* Vol. 2. Cleveland: Arthur H. Clark Co., 1904.

Vestal, Stanley. *Kit Carson.* Boston: Houghton Mifflin, 1928.

Wallace, Ernest, with E. Adamson Hoebel. *The Comanches, Lords of the South Plains.* Norman: University of Oklahoma Press, 1952.

Wharton, Clarence. *Satanta, The Great Chief of the Kiowas.* Dallas: Banks and Upshaw, 1935.

White, Owen P. *The Autobiography of a Durable Sinner.* New York: G. P. Putnam's Sons, 1942.

———. *Texas: An Informal Biography.* New York: G. P. Putnam's Sons, 1945.

Wilbarger, J. W. *Indian Depredations of Texas.* Austin: Steck Co., 1935.

INDEX